WET

30-DAY DEEP DIVE INTO
Sensual Bliss and Feminine Pleasure

LADY SHEPSA JONES

WET: 30-Day Deep Dive into Sensual Bliss and Feminine Pleasure

Paperback (ISBN): 978-1-7356014-3-4
Ebook (ISBN): 978-1-7356014-4-1

Illustrations copyright 2021 *Tameka Jones*
Illustrated by *Alisha Hagelin*
Julia "Nubian-Bey Goolsby of Blaque Penn Comix
Cover Photos copyright 2021 *Tameka Jones*
Photos taken by *Karyn Westbrooks*
Cover and Interior Design: *Marites Bautista*

CONTENTS

DEDICATION

This book is dedicated to women everywhere who know that they deserve a life of bliss, sexiness and full body orgasms.

INTRODUCTION

On Being WET...

On August 7, 2020, Cardi B. and Meghan Thee Stallion released a controversial song by the name of WAP, which is an acronym for Wet-Ass Pussy. The world literally went crazy. Conservatives branded it "disgusting and vile", and one Congressional hopeful claimed it made him want to "pour holy water" in his ears. Others in the media embraced it as a message of feminine empowerment and sexual liberation. Despite the bleeding ears of conservatives, WAP has gone on to break records and go quintuple platinum.

Seeing the outrage of people, particularly men, on my social media timeline made me laugh. *Would you rather have Dry-Ass Pussy?* I wanted to know. For one thing all the controversy showed me that folks are still afraid of the pussy and women speaking freely about their pleasure (and God forbid anyone dare mention lubrication).

I believe a wet-ass pussy is a healthy pussy, and we should all proudly be connected to our WAP! In this book, however, we are going to expand the idea of wetness. More than just vaginal lubrication, wetness is a way of being. It's a vibration.

When I'm *wet*, I'm dripping in sensual bliss and feminine pleasure. I'm easily aroused by the sensation of opening up to receive ALL the goodness of life! This goodness looks like many different things, from a good nap, a beautiful bouquet of pink roses, a hot bath with lavender oil and sea salt, some yummy Ethiopian food, or me riding in ecstasy on top of my lover. Whatever the experience, I allow myself to be penetrated. I hold my quaking legs open and receive every sensation, every ripple, every charge. I am in tune with the energy flowing in and through me. I allow myself to receive all the joy, ecstasy, and every good thing.

Being *wet*, however, is not just about fulfilling what some may mislabel as hedonistic desires. When I am *wet*, I also receive my emotions that don't feel so good because, after all, where would the light be without the dark? I allow myself to love and accept all of me. If sadness, worry, fear, or anger decide they want to pull up a seat at the table, I do not ignore them. I treat them with respect. I make them a plate too. I witness them. I do not repress, squelch or suppress. I know they also have something important to say.

I know that, in times of contrast, something is being birthed within me. There is always a lesson, and it is a gift if I am still and quiet enough to receive it. I allow myself to also be *wet* with tears. I allow myself to be cracked open to myself. I allow myself to marvel at my own ability to heal, grow, be a mess, get messy and expand beyond what I ever thought possible before.

This ability to expand is a secret power of wetness. It is an internal expansion that floods my entire being and spills outward. I am so aroused and turned on from within that I do not necessarily need others to play in my water park. This wetness can benefit my lovers, and there is no doubt that I thoroughly enjoy sharing the gift of my juiciness with those that are worthy.

But I know more than anything I am my own lover first. I know more than anything I choose me first. I know more than anything I am seeking to please me and pleasure me first. This is the journey of wetness: that others may swim in my overflow, but I marinate in the cup. When I walk by, you may touch the hem of my garment and become drenched! That my mere presence would inspire others to get *wet* too.

This is what I want for you, dear goddess. This is why I created this book. I want you dripping *wet*. In fact, we will go on a 30-day journey together in which you will be swimming in a sea of your wetness. I want you to know you are worthy of feeling good. I want you to know that, no matter what is going on in your life or the world, pleasure is your birthright. I want you to know that no matter how dried up and stressed out you may feel from day to day, there is an oasis ready to hydrate you.

I had to discover this oasis for myself. I was once Sahara desert dry. Here's a bit about how I discovered the power of my own wetness.

My Journey to Wetness

The year was 2010. It was Memorial Day weekend and I was childfree. After separating from my then-husband, I had recently moved into my apartment and was on the road to self-discovery. This road to self-discovery led me on an actual road trip to Washington, DC., with a sista friend of mine to attend the Bellydancers Of Colors Expo run by dancer, chef, and holistic healer Dr. Sunyatta Amen.

I had been taking bellydance classes weekly at the local YMCA and had bought Dr. Sunyatta's Bellydance DVD the previous summer at a local festival in Brooklyn. I loved seeing beautiful Black women sway their hips and flow with their sensual energy. There was a gap between me and my sexual energy. We were not united: more like long-lost cousins who knew we were related but never really met before. We sort of knew what each other looked like. We wanted to hang out and connect, but it hadn't happened yet.

Bellydancing became the way for me to begin to open this door of connection. It became an outlet for me to heal after leaving my marriage and needing to discover who I was as a woman. I had been a virgin until I was 22 years old and married the first man I ever had sex with. Here I was at 29, getting a divorce and needing to explore my sensual self that I had repressed for so long.

The expo was amazing. We danced from morning until night, not only with sessions in bellydance, but we also had "Bellydancehall," where we did bellydance moves to Jamaican reggae music. We did yoga classes, burlesque workshops, Afro-Cuban Folkloric dance classes, booty-popping classes, and Afro-Brazilian dance classes. Dr. Amen also taught a session called "Sexual Kung Fu." It was this class that opened the way to my wetness...

In this class, I learned that there were ancient secrets (thousands of years old) that women practiced and which made them "immortal." Though they aged, they kept the vitality, juiciness, and sexual health of a much younger woman. I was exposed to the concept of sacred sexuality - the philosophy that sexuality is spiritual and sex can be a prayer. I was introduced to the teachings of a man called Mantak Chia, who was a Taoist master and brought many of these concepts to the Western world. I also discovered the jade egg and bought my first one.

The jade egg is an ancient secret tool, once only known by the women of the royal court in China. Using the egg was one of their secrets to immortality and sexual vitality. It kept them wet!

I remember the first time I awkwardly inserted my jade egg inside my *yoni* (Sanskrit word for vagina meaning sacred space and divine passage), aka *vajajay*. I was standing on top of the bed in my hotel room, hoping it wouldn't plop out, but making sure it would have a soft landing if it did. I could only hold the egg inside my yoni for a few moments before feeling it slide and exit. Plop it went, down on the bed!

Despite my beginner efforts, I was excited that I found a practice I could use to heal and awaken my sexual energy. With the name Mantak Chia in my mind I went on a search for his books and began a serious, independent study and practice of these ancient Taoists techniques of sexual alchemy.

Around this time, I was also hanging with the gods and goddesses in Brooklyn, NY - men and women who knew they were divine. One group called Goddess Herstory would host events celebrating the divine feminine and sacred sexuality. I took an erotic dance and pole class taught by a dear sista-friend that eventually led to me doing a couple of sensual dance performances. I went from long skirts and headwraps to booty shorts and fishnet stockings!

I spent months and months working through the complex and dense exercises in Mantak Chia's book *Healing Love through the Tao: Cultivating Female Sexual Energy*. In time, something began to unlock. The floodgates to my sexual energy became open, and I was wet all over.

This sexual awakening came after years of conditioning from society and religion that sexuality was dangerous. As a Black woman growing up in the 'hood, I had constant reminders that my job was not to become a "statistic," an unwed teenage mother like some members of my family and community. The message I was fed was to keep your legs closed until you're married because the Bible says so, boys are bad and dangerous and only want to use you for sex, and if you become a teenage mother, you will have failed at life.

This messaging was so strong I never dated in high school or college, and that was how I was still a virgin at 22. I married the first and only man I had ever had sex with. Two years into the marriage, having given birth to my son, I knew my ex-husband was not the man for me. I had spent all my life being the "good girl" for everyone else; I needed to discover the "woman" for me. (Anyone struggling with a "good girl" complex should also check out my book, *Nice For What?! How To Go From Being A Good Girl To A Badass Goddess*.)

Despite being virginal most of my life, I had intense sexual energy that I had been hiding under the covers since middle school, where I would rendezvous with imaginary lovers and crushes. My hands would pleasure me as I imagined an erotic sexual life I never had. Due to religious influence, I felt guilt and shame around masturbation and continued to stuff my sexual energy deep inside me.

This sexual healing and deep dive had been 29 years in the making, and I felt like I had hit the jackpot. I finally found the answer to what I had been seeking in sacred sexuality. Yes, I could be deeply spiritual *and* deeply sexual, and in fact, the more I opened up to my orgasmic nature, the more I opened up to Spirit.

As I devoured the ancient practices of Taoism and Tantra, I soon had a toolbox of practices that brought healing, wholeness, pleasure, and bliss. I transformed from being rigid and repressed to being juicy, flexible, and sensual. No matter what was going on in the outer world or my life, I could always turn to my practices to ground myself and find wholeness.

I started to attract different types of lovers. At the beginning of my sexual journey, after leaving my marriage, I felt awkward, insecure, and unconfident. While I did enjoy many of my sexual experiences with my new partners, it was rather ordinary.

As I deepened my practices of sacred sexuality, the type of partners I manifested transformed and the type of sex I had transformed. I have included a story I wrote about one of my first juicy sacred sexual encounters at the end of this book. I began to attract men who either knew of these practices or were naturally adept and open. My sexual experiences became places of healing and transformation. I had mystical and spiritual experiences in the bedroom. I was able to circulate my energy to experience full-body orgasms. I went into trance during sex and found myself having out-of-body experiences and speaking in tongues. The two parts of myself, the sexual and the spiritual were now one.

As I walked this road, many of my friends began to notice my transformation. I was free. I was happy, and my sensuality and confidence were through the roof. In August of 2012, a friend of mine was hosting a health and wellness event for women. She asked me to present a workshop on sacred sexuality to the group. This was the beginning of my work as a sacred sexuality teacher and coach.

The Sacred Sex Teacher Is Born

Being the nerd that I am, I had no problem going over much of the dense material in Mantak Chia's and other Taoist and Tantra teachers' books. I knew, however, that many of the women in my community may not be as patient with the material. I wanted to create a way for women who looked like me to be introduced to these practices in a way that felt relatable, and they could consume in chunks.

In 2014 I traveled to Asheville, North Carolina, and studied the Healing Love practices with Michael Winn, the founder of Healing Tao USA. He co-wrote many books with Mantak Chia. The retreat was co-taught with Minke De Vos, one of the first people ever certified by Mantak Chia. This experience further solidified my practices, and from here, I was inspired to create the first incarnation of this work called Sacred Sex Bootcamp. (I then later changed the name to Sensual Goddess Bootcamp because anything with the word "sex" gets flagged on social media.)

This program was a 30-day coaching program in which participants received a different sacred sex exercise every day for 30 days grouped into four weekly themes. Back then, I liked the idea of it being a "bootcamp" because it was intensive. It was designed to give women practical ways to apply the teachings of sacred sex into their life with hands-on practice and exercises in bite-sized pieces. I had been a public school classroom teacher for nine years, so I knew that learning must be hands-on; it cannot remain an intellectual exercise.

It is not enough to just read that you are a reflection of divine feminine energy and that your nature is to be multi-orgasmic; you need to get that into your body. You need to practice it and explore it. I've seen many so-called Tantra teachers espouse advice that is as generic as store-brand cereal and popular books that regurgitate advice you could easily google. This is not what you will find here. The practices I share with you are grounded and specific while also being juicy and fun.

Well over 300 hundred women around the world have experienced the power of the Bootcamp during the past seven years. Now, in 2021, I have decided to change the name of the program, expand it and bring everything together into a book so that it can reach more women.

Why Pleasure Matters Now More Than Ever

In 2020 as a global community, we experienced an unprecedented pandemic that shook our world to its core. Many of us have found ourselves spending more time at home than ever, and many of us feel more isolated than ever. It is my hope that *WET: 30 Day Deep Dive into Sensual Bliss and Feminine Pleasure* can help women find joy, bliss, and juiciness within themselves. Having a host of practices to drive off pandemic fatigue and blues can be one of many tools to help all of us get through this challenging time.

While in 2017, I did eventually travel to spend time in Thailand studying the Tao-Tantric Arts with Shashi Solluna and Minke de Vos, I had spent many years in my home temple, located in Bed-Stuy, Brooklyn, doing this work. Unlike many of the European women I studied with who had the privilege to travel about the world finding themselves, I was a single mother with a son and a job. It took three years to get my ass to Thailand to complete the program after meeting Minke in 2014, but the work I did on my own was no less important.

I want all women to know that you can find the Goddess and her powers of wetness where you are right now. It doesn't matter if you are in the midst of a messy divorce; if your baby daddy is getting on your damn nerves; if you are riding the subway or on the bus; or if you are busting your ass in school or at work.

The medicine is not just for the privileged or those who can spend years wandering through ashrams in India.

This medicine is sacred, and it is for all of us.

How to Use this Book

This book contains 30 exercises divided into four weeks with two bonus exercises to round it out to a full 30. Each day, there are journal reflection questions to help you process this work. Be sure to complete them; you may want to get a journal just for this experience. Each week there is a different theme that connects the exercises for that week.

Our themes are:

- Pleasure
- Juicy
- Sexy
- Orgasmic

The exercises are designed to go in order. The only time an exercise should be skipped is if you cannot do it because you are on your cycle. I have created a special set of exercises women can do who are menstruating. You will find those at the end of the book. I've also included as a bonus a description of a sacred sexual ritual you can do with a lover. To inspire your lovemaking, I close this book with a short story I wrote about my first time having sacred sex.

While this is designed to be a 30-day deep dive, you are encouraged to move at your own pace. If you miss a day or two here and there, that is fine. However, part of my intention of creating daily exercises is because I want women to find space for daily sensual self-care. I want women to prioritize their pleasure and sexual sovereignty. This can be accomplished by taking 30 days to dive deep into these practices. Plus, by accumulating energy, rather than stopping and starting, you will get the maximum benefit.

I will also tell you that, while I have broken down these exercises and sacred sex concepts into bite-sized pieces, it is not watered down. You are about to experience a lot of content. It is an immersion! I've had clients tell me this can be a 3- or 6-month course.

This is why it's not only a book but also a coaching program. You will get the maximum benefit of this book by taking advantage of the live calls, workshops, videos, and meditations that I've created to support the work in this book. Please visit my website www.letgoletgoddess. com to sign up for the bonuses that support this book if you haven't done so already.

While I studied many of these concepts and practices on my own, my understanding and experience flourished when I began to work with teachers and masters who have been doing this for decades. To truly understand this work at a deep level, you need a teacher. I am grateful for the many teachers I've had that allows me to integrate these teachings.

These teachings are fundamentally rooted in Taoist concepts and practices, with some Tantric philosophy and practice weaved in but it is largely Taoist. Most of my teachers carry on the lineage from Mantak Chia, who is the creator of Universal Healing Tao and the Healing Love practices. Taoism is a philosophy that comes from ancient China and is based on the concept of the Tao. The word "Tao" translates to mean "the way" and it is about living in a way that is in harmony with nature.

Tantra has become a controversial and hotly debated topic in the last few years. This is mainly because the Neo-Tantra movement has been seen as a bastardization of classical Tantra that places an overemphasis on sex. I, too, have had a bad taste left in my mouth because of many Neo-Tantra techniques, which are more like psycho-sexual practices, with a little spiritual philosophy thrown in. There is often an overemphasis on sex, yet the real roots of Tantra embody much more. I have also seen many people tout Taoist concepts and practices and mislabel them as Tantra. Upon seeing their explanation of these concepts and practices, it is always clear to me that their understanding is very superficial. So I always say I am Tantric in philosophy but more Taoist in practice. The Taoist teachings, for me, are much more authentic, less watered down and less problematic than those you may receive from many Neo-Tantra teachers.

Many of these concepts may be new to you. I invite you to go slowly and get on some live coaching calls so any questions you have may be answered. This is designed to be a fun exploration so, don't worry about getting it wrong. It is called a practice for a reason. Each time you do a particular exercise, your experience may be different. I am still learning new things and having new insights. I still attend workshops, work with teachers, and practice with sisters from my Tao-Tantric Arts training.

Be patient with yourself and allow it to be a journey of discovery and exploration. You are connecting to traditions that are thousands of years old, joining a circle of women across time and cultures who have found healing in these practices.

While I have done my best to preserve the integrity of the Taoist lineage, I have also infused my modern Black girl magic into this work. This medicine is infused with tones of Lady Shepsa and what I've learned over the last seven years from sharing these teachings with women in my community.

I welcome you to this dance, dear goddess. May this medicine assist you in being WET! May you be drenched and drowning in sensual bliss and feminine pleasure until your cup runneth over...

"Bring a bucket and a mop..."
—WAP, Cardi B.

WEEK 1:

PLEASURE

Introduction

> *"To be sensual, I think, is to respect and rejoice in the force of life, of life itself, and to be present in all that one does, from the effort of loving to the breaking of bread."*
> **—James Baldwin**

Do you prioritize your pleasure? Or do you put it on the backburner? Right now, I want you to think about one of the most pleasurable experiences you've ever had. Go ahead. Stop, close your eyes, and imagine it. Feel it in your body. It's a judgment-free zone. Close your eyes, take a deep breath, and go....

How did that feel? Was it easy or hard to go there? Now I want you to imagine what life would be if you felt like that every day. Take that feeling and times it by 100, 1,000, 10,000. Can you be open to receiving that? The amount of pleasure we can receive is infinite! Yet we very rarely invite pleasure in. This week is going to change that.

We will begin our deep dive by connecting to our pleasure through exploring the five senses. We will delve very deeply into the sensation of touch. We shall lay hands on our bodies to heal ourselves and experience the pleasure of our own temples. As James Baldwin said, *being sensual is about being present.* I invite you to stop cutting yourself off from what you are sensing. We dumb our senses down to numb ourselves from the harsh realities of the world. Racism, crime, police brutality, poverty, the pandemic, etc., can leave us feeling overwhelmed. At times wearing protective armor is necessary, but we also need to have a sacred space to let our guard down. It is time to open up our senses to pleasure!

Opening the Way to Pleasure

To help us open up to receive more pleasure, we will begin with a practice called *The Healing Wands Of Light* that I've also dubbed the *Open To Pleasure Meditation.* This is important pre-work that we need to do before we delve into the exercises for the week. We will learn the six Taoist healing sounds and use them to release negative energy that is trapped in our womb. Our womb is a powerful center of transformation and manifestation. When we have a healthy connection to our womb, we feel grounded, centered, sensual and creative.

However, when we have experienced traumas and negative experiences around our feminine self and sexuality, this energy can get stuck in the womb. This stuck energy can be the cause of womb diseases and problems like painful menses, fibroid tumors, PCOS, infertility, etc. It is essential to release this energy from the womb prior to cultivating our sexual energy (and continuously during our healing journey).

Women who've had hysterectomies can still do this meditation as the psychic or energetic womb is still there.

Along with this practice being able to heal our wombs, it helps bring us into emotional balance through energetic transmutation. When beginning to cultivate sexual energy, it is first important to clear out negative or stuck energy that causes emotional imbalances.

Sexual energy has two main properties: *to bind* and *to amplify*. Failure to cleanse out toxic emotions will cause the sexual energy you circulate to bind to the dormant, negative energy you're carrying and amplify it. For example, you could find yourself feeling passionately angry, sad, worried, etc., or be on an emotional rollercoaster if you raise your sexual energy while holding emotional imbalances.

This is why oftentimes when in an intimate relationship with someone, our issues come out so strongly. You may find yourself acting jealous and doing behaviors that seem out of your control. You wonder why you have no handle over your emotions as they pendulum back and forth from ecstasy to despair.

Today we often laugh at someone behaving this way and call them "dickmatized" or "pussy-whipped." We might even have been the wild and crazy one ready to slash tires while on a tirade (Look, there's no judgment from me if you did it, girl). This is because the sexual energy you have exchanged with your partner has bonded to your dormant negative emotional patterns, and they are now being amplified. Sexual energy is like gasoline, throw it on a small fire, and it's going to burn more. The answer, of course, is to focus on letting go of the patterns and cleansing your energy. It's not necessarily about your partner; he or she is just the catalyst. One way to do this is through *qi gong*. Consider it like the water that stops your fire from getting out of control.

Qi gong or *chi gong* is an ancient Taoist moving meditation that helps to cultivate, cleanse and fortify energy in our body. *Qi*, meaning life force, is the energy that Taoist believe runs through all living things. It is the energy that animates the Universe. *Gong* means the cultivation of skill. When we do *qi gong*, we are cultivating our powerful life force energy.

The healing sounds in *qi gong* are connected to major organs (like the kidneys, liver, heart, etc.) and their various pathways, called meridians, that run through the body. These are the same meridians that acupuncturists use, inserting needles into specific points that lie on these meridians to bring energetic balance to the body.

Each organ is also connected to an element, color, emotion, and season. Through doing the healing sound for each organ, you help to air out negative emotions and stagnant energy. The sounds act as a ventilation system, so your organs don't "overheat". I suggest using the healing sounds on a regular basis if you'd like to cultivate your sexual energy. This will help you maintain emotional balance as you do this deep work.

It is also not that these emotions are "bad". I believe in emotional intelligence and that our emotions are visitors who come to teach us something. However, sometimes these visitors outstay their welcome and need some assistance in leaving. We use *qi gong* to become alchemists who transform negative or stuck emotions into gold (positive emotions).

When we release pent-up, negative emotions, we free up energy that we can use for our healing.

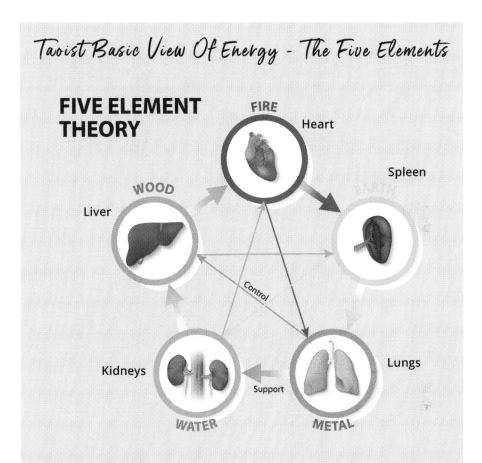

Taoist Basic View Of Energy - The Five Elements

FIVE ELEMENT THEORY

FIRE — Heart
Spleen
WOOD — Liver
Control
Kidneys
Support
Lungs
WATER
METAL

Taoists see all of life coming from an undifferentiated whole which they call "The Tao." Out of this oneness comes *yin* (feminine energy) and *yang* (masculine energy), which are the poles of this unified whole. *Yin* and *yang* symbolize the creation process through interaction of these bipolar forces. Feminine and masculine energy "make love" to birth life.

Out of *yin* and *yang* are birthed the five elements and the five ways that energy flows:

- Fire rises
- Earth is stabilizing and centering
- Metal solidifies
- Water sinks
- Wood expands

The general energy of the body is broken down into five strands of *qi*. These five elements are connected to specific organs and their respective meridians that run through the body. In Chinese medicine, an organ is not just a physical organ but an energy pathway with many correspondences.

Here is a list of the major organs used in Chinese medicine and their various correspondences. We will move through these in our Open to Pleasure meditation.

The Five Organs and their Healing Sounds

1. **Lungs.** The lungs are connected to the element of metal and the season of fall. Just as the trees release their leaves in autumn to prepare for winter hibernation, the ability to let go is key for the metal element. When we are unable to let go, we may experience excess grief or feelings of loss that lead to sadness. Making the healing sound that corresponds to the lungs helps us release sadness, grief, mourning, and loss. Instead, we

cultivate feelings of inspiration, self-esteem, integrity, courage, respect, and the ability to let go. The color for the lungs is white, which reflects purity, a property of metal. The healing sound is SSSSSSSSS.

2. **Kidneys.** After fall comes winter, which brings us to the water element and its organ: the kidneys. The kidneys are considered the battery of the body, where *jing* or sexual essence comes from (we'll discuss this in a later section). The color is blue, like the deep ocean. When the kidneys are imbalanced, we may experience feelings of fear and loneliness. The water element also connects to trauma and the autonomic nervous system. When we use the healing sound for the kidneys, it helps us to release fear and our traumas. Instead, we cultivate peace, willpower, faith, and actualization. The healing sound is TCHOOOO, which is made with pursed lips like you're blowing something out.

3. **Liver.** After the rest and hibernation of the winter, energy begins to rise with the spring, bringing us the wood element and liver organ. The color is green, just like fresh spring grass. Liver energy is important for sexual arousal: a man's morning "wood" reflects this energy. Making the healing sound for the liver helps us release anger, frustration, jealousy, and resentment. We then cultivate kindness, relaxation, creative vision, and hope. The healing sound for the liver is SHHHHHH.

4. **Heart.** From spring, summer comes and brings the heat. This is the time of the fire element and the heart. The color is red like, well, fire, of course. The heart is where *shen* or spirit is located

and is considered to be the "king" of the organs. When we make the healing sound, we release feeling overly excited, anxious, hastiness, violence, bitterness, arrogance, and impatience. We then feel love, happiness, joy, and compassion. The sound of the heart is HAAAAAAAW.

5. **Spleen.** In the Taoist system, we recognize late summer as a season and it is connected with the earth element and the spleen. Think of harvest time, when the earth is yielding her pumpkins and vegetable bounty. The earth is also considered feminine, and earth energy is important for women. The color is yellow, like a beautiful sunset. When we make the healing sound for the spleen, we release worry, anxiety, self-doubt, obsession, over-thinking, and neediness. Instead, we cultivate stability, security, contentment, balance, groundedness, and trust. The sound is WOOOOOOO.

Triple Heater. Triple Heater is the final sound, and though not an organ per se, it is connected to the heart and fire element. We use the sound of the triple heater to bring down excess heat, empty the mind of mental clutter and bring clarity and balance. The sound is HEEEEE.

Meditation Prep

1. Ensure you have a quiet space (put the kids to bed, turn off the TV, silence your phone, etc.).

2. Dress in loose, comfortable clothes; all-white is preferred as it neutralizes negative energy and inspires feelings of peace.

3. Have candles, incense, or anything else ready that helps put you in a relaxed mood. You can burn sage, palo santo, or other incense to cleanse negative energy.

4. Have a journal ready to record insights you receive after the meditation. Before meditation, list things that you feel are holding you back from experiencing more pleasure on a daily basis.

Wands of Light Instructions

1. Most Taoist meditations are done sitting up with your back straight in a chair. Find a comfortable sitting position; in a chair is preferred, with your feet flat on the floor.

2. Take a few deep breaths and imagine roots from the soles of your feet going into the earth sipping up the *qi* from the earth. Feel yourself ground into the earth.

3. Raise your arms to the heavens and call on your spirit guides, helpers, ancestors, etc., to assist you in this release.

4. Ask that your hands become wands of light, and imagine wands extending from each finger, glowing with healing energy.

5. Slowly bring your hands down to your lap.

6. Take one hand and make a clockwise circle in between your legs on the floor. You are creating a vortex in the earth to transmute the energy you are going to release.

7. Return your hands to your lap and imagine the wands are now white, relating to the metal element and the lungs.

8. Take your hands and breathe in deeply while making a sweeping up motion. Imagine your wands of light are penetrating deeply into your womb, ovaries, etc., and breaking up the negative energy there.

9. Then you will place your hands in front of your womb, palms facing down. Hold your breath for a few seconds while simultaneously squeezing the internal muscles of your yoni (do a Kegel, imagine you are stopping your urine mid-flow).

10. When you release your breath, you will use the healing sound for the lungs, which is SSSSSSSSS. As you do this, imagine that smoky air representing toxic *qi* is exiting your mouth and going into the vortex in the earth to be recycled. Release the sadness, grief, and feelings of loss from your womb space

11. Then imagine glowing white balls of white light representing the purity of the metal element. Place this energy into your womb. Feel inspiration, courage, integrity, and the power to let go.

12. You will repeat these steps for the rest of the five elements, using their respective healing sounds, color, and emotions.

13. You will end with the sound for the Triple Heater, HEEEEEEE, while imagining the wands are now clear crystals releasing any energy from your womb that doesn't belong to you.

14. End with your hands on your womb smiling and sending golden light there, representing the power of alchemy.

Items Needed for Pleasure Week

- A natural massage oil (coconut, almond, grapeseed oil, etc.)

- Natural sea or epsom salt (pink Himalayan salt is a good choice, but any will do)

- Organic apple cider vinegar

- Lavender essential oil

- White flowers (you don't need these until the end of the week)

- Purifying incense such as sage, palo santo, rosemary, or frankincense

- A blue candle and a white candle

Week 1: Pleasure

Quote for the Week:

"Pleasure is not frivolous. It is not extra. It is not dessert. Pleasure is the main course. Fatten yourself on pleasure, and you will malnourish pain."

—Lady Shepsa Jones

Day 1

Intention: Realize the infinite amount of ways you can conjure up pleasure.

Welcome Goddess,

Today starts the beginning of your journey into more pleasure! We are no longer putting our pleasure on the back burner. We are going to please ourselves first! Nourish ourselves first. Pleasure is medicine. As we begin to explore our pleasure, let us focus on what ignites us!

Our brains are wired for pleasure. We need to experience pleasure on a regular basis to be healthy and functional human beings. Brain scientists have linked pleasure as being essential for overall happiness and satisfaction in life. In fact, scientists have discovered that both human and animal brains are hardwired with pleasure centers.

These pleasure pathways have to be stimulated sufficiently by serotonin, dopamine and other neurotransmitters if the organisms (us) are to function optimally. Pleasurable activities (such as eating good food or having enjoyable sex) can actually reduce stress by inhibiting anxiety responses in the brain.

In the spirit of the Law of Attraction that states *"like attracts like,"* what we focus on expands. We are going to focus on the myriad of ways we experience pleasure.

Exercise:

Make a list of 100 things that bring you pleasure. Yup **100**!! Don't think about it too much. Just write. Try setting a timer and see how far you can get in 15 mins. Your list should be short and straight to the point: no paragraphs or long explanations. Get into your instinctual self; you may discover things you forgot about. Close your eyes. Take a few moments to breathe deeply and begin writing. If you don't get to 100 in your first shot, come back to it throughout the day. See if you can have 100 items by the end of the day.

Example:

1. Summertime
2. Chocolate
3. Jamaica
4. Chai latte tea
5. His tongue
6. Cookies and cream ice cream
7. Coconut water
8. Ethiopian food
9. Jazz
10. Naps

Got it? Have fun thinking about what gives you pleasure.

Journal Reflection

1. Was it easy or hard for you to come up with one hundred things that give you pleasure? If it was challenging, reflect on why.

_____

_____

_____

_____

_____

2. Discuss any ways that you are damming up your pleasure in your life. How can you carve out more time for pleasure?

_____

_____

_____

_____

_____

Day 2

Intention: Unite our pleasure with our senses.

Our pleasure is a window to our sensuality. We use our five senses on a daily basis to communicate with the world and take in information from our environment. Our eyes alert us to danger. Our taste allows us to enjoy our food. Being able to feel lets us know if something is wrong in our body.

Today, however, we are going to begin bathing our five senses in pleasure! We are going to be purposeful about opening up our five senses to delight. This is being sensual, taking your time to feel, taste, touch, smell, and hear.

Try out **one** of the ideas under each sense. To really indulge this experience, we will only cover three senses today. Tomorrow we will do the remaining two.

Exercise: (Choose one idea from each section)

1. **Smell**

   Did you know smell is one of the oldest senses? Smell is also the only sense we can't stop doing. We can close our eyes, plug our ears, but must breathe. However, very often, we don't put intention into this sense. We will smell with intention today.

   Discover a scent today that intoxicates your nose.

   • Go to a bath and body shop, or try out a new perfume or essential oil. Breathe it in, close your eyes. If you feel up to it, treat yourself and buy it!

- Put on a favorite perfume or body oil. Close your eyes and take in the fragrance. You can also place it on your body and have a lover smell you.

- Cook or bake something that will make your house smell delicious. Indulge in the luscious aroma. Notice how the smell whets your appetite.

2. **Taste**

Of the five classic senses, taste is the oldest. Ancient organisms began swimming toward "tasty" nutrients in primordial oceans billions of years ago. Today, you will "swim" toward your own tasty treats!

Devour something delectable.

- Buy yourself your favorite sweet treat or savory snack. Close your eyes while you eat it and merge with the taste. Let your whole body become the tongue.

- Taste something new! Sample something you've never tasted before. Allow the new flavor to ripple throughout your body. You can go to a restaurant or store and ask for a recommendation.

- Cook or buy your favorite food. Eat slowly, savoring each bite. Close your eyes while chewing and fully merge with the experience.

Bonus: Taste your lover. Try anointing your lover's body with honey (be sure to taste the honey first). Allow your tongue to slide and taste their flavor mingled with some extra sweetness. Switch!

3. **See**

   For humans, sight is king and is the primary sense we use to interact with the world. However, we often take it for granted. Today you will open your eyes and truly see.

   Allow your eyes to feast on beauty.

   - Feast with your eyes. Take in the beautiful people around you. Find someone attractive? Allow your eyes to drink them in. Pretend the eyes are straws and sip them up. (No stalking, though, giggle.)

   - Go for a walk and look at nature. Allow yourself to admire the beauty of the natural world. Try visiting the park, take in the sky, sun, grass and trees with your eyes.

   - Notice colors. Choose your favorite color and notice how many things you see in that color throughout the day. See if you discover any new shades you like. Go to a store in person or online and buy a scarf, shirt, skirt, or dress of that color.

   Bonus: Invite a lover over for a *Being Seen Ritual.* Have your lover stand in front of you in silence (naked if they are comfortable) and allow yourself to *truly see* them, take in all their beauty. Afterward, share with them what you find beautiful about their body. Then switch. You can also choose to be seen first since this exercise can be very vulnerable. We often don't see others or allow ourselves to be seen. End with a melting hug.

Journal Reflection

1. On a daily basis, are you usually connected to your senses? What are some of the ways you have dulled or numbed your senses in the past?

    _____

    _____

    _____

    _____

    _____

2. What was it like to sensually focus on smell, taste, and sight? What did you discover?

    _____

    _____

    _____

    _____

    _____

Day 3

Intention: Unite our pleasure with our senses part 2.

Today we will complete opening up our senses to pleasure. Enjoy!

1. **Hear**

   Hearing is believed to be the last sense to evolve. Can you imagine primal creatures first discovering this sense? The joy and rapture of hearing rainfall, waves of the ocean, or the wind? Today you allow yourself to hear like it's the first time.

   Listen to something that makes you feel devilishly divine.

   - Play your favorite sensual song and dance like a sex goddess. Notice how the sexy notes make you feel in your body

   - Discover a new piece of music. Ask a friend to recommend their favorite sexy song. Give your friend a recommendation too.

   - Talk to someone whose voice you love. Close your eyes and just listen to how they speak. Be bathed in their sound.

   Bonus: Go to a sound bath, either in-person or online. Sound baths are meditation events where participants lie in relaxation while someone plays crystal bowls or gongs. The sound bath helps to clear negative energy, promotes relaxation and stimulates the parasympathetic nervous system.

2. **Feel**

   Touch is the first sense that humans develop in the embryo. This sense develops at around eight weeks. In fact, babies that are not touched and held will fail to thrive and can actually die. Our skin is the largest organ in our body, yet many of us are touch-starved. Touch starvation was a huge issue in American culture, even prior to the COVID-19 pandemic. The need to social distance and be quarantined at home has made lack of touch a real mental health phenomenon.

As a massage therapist, I know the power of touch is therapeutic and naturally healing. Healing touch helps to reduce stress and even lessen future stress. It boosts the immune system, increases circulation, improves cognitive function, and boosts self-esteem. It naturally lowers cortisol, the stress hormone, and releases oxytocin, the love hormone.

Touch will play a big part in our 30-day journey. Let's start receiving loving touch today!

Indulge in the sensation of touch.

- Wear something soft and silky. Allow it to caress your body. Close your eyes and feel into the sensation.

- Sleep naked on soft sheets. Allow yourself to feel the freedom of no clothes while asleep and the caress of the bedding on your body.

- Have a melting hug. Get or give a good hug from someone today. The minimum embrace time is 30 seconds. Allow yourself to melt into the other person.

Bonus: 6th Sense. As women, we are uniquely connected to our intuition. Part of reconnecting to our femininity is to open our awareness to our 6th sense. Intuition is that part of us that knows without knowing; it is our gut instinct, the voice whispering to us in the back of our mind.

Listen to that voice and allow your intuition to bring you a new sensual experience.

Tip: Set the intention to have a new sensual experience today. State it out loud. Expect it to show up. Watch what happens. It may look like going on a walk and discovering a new shop that has yummy treats, sexy clothing, or delectable smelling oils. It could look like connecting to a friend you haven't spoken to in a while. The possibilities are endless! Open up to receive.

Journal Reflection

1. How was it to focus sensually on hearing, feeling, and your intuition?

   _____

   _____

   _____

   _____

   _____

2. What sensual experience did you manifest with your sixth sense? (If nothing yet, give it time.) How can you open to receive more sensuality in your life on a daily basis?

   _____

   _____

   _____

   _____

   _____

Day 4

Intention: To indulge in the pleasure of touch.

For our pleasure exercise today, we are going to go deeper into the sense of touch. Of all the senses, touch is the most controversial and the most ignored. As women, we may have had times that someone touched us without our consent. We may have been violated through touch and thus have either shut this sense down or have very strong protective barriers up.

If there was a time in your life when someone touched you inappropriately or without permission, try using these exercises as a way to reclaim the power of touch to heal, not to kill the spirit. If you need to release the experience, try using the healing sounds while sending light to the area that was violated.

You can explore the pleasure of touch by getting a full body massage. You can:

A. Book a professional therapist if time and money allow.

B. Ask a friend or lover to massage you.

C. Give yourself a full body massage.

Tips for self-massage:

- Use a natural oil like coconut, almond, jojoba, or grapeseed oil.

- Try adding a scent like lavender or eucalyptus to relax tired muscles.

- Self-massage can be very healing and stimulating. It is fine to touch and rub your own body with loving hands.

- Try moving fingers in a circular motion to circulate the energy. Start at the bottoms of your feet and move up your entire body: legs, knees, thighs, stomach, chest, arms, neck, scalp, etc. (Moving in this direction is raising and expanding your energy).

- Finish the massage by lightly stroking your fingertips up your body, starting at the soles of your feet. Pay special attention to stroke up your inner leg and thigh up to your yoni. This is where the *yin* (feminine energy) energy meridians are found.

Tips:

- If receiving a massage, remember to ask for what you want. Use your voice to let out sounds of pleasure.

- Try touching yourself or being touched with different things like feathers, ice, warm gemstones, etc.

Journal Reflection

1. What did it feel like to be touched with loving intention, either from your hands or someone else's?

_____

_____

_____

_____

_____

2. Reflect on the power of "laying on of hands." How can you touch or receive more touch?

_____

_____

_____

_____

_____

Day 5

Intention: Pleasure and heal your breasts through breast breathing and massage.

The practice you will do today is foundational to healing with sexual energy and opening up to deeper orgasms. The ancient Taoists called the breasts, "bells of love." The breasts unlock the key to female orgasm and having an open, loving heart. Working with our breasts–heart center opens the way for us to heal our womb and connect with our yoni.

There is a direct link between the breasts and womb that nursing mothers can attest to. When a mother nurses her baby, the hormone oxytocin is released, which helps to bond the baby to the mother and also causes the uterus to contract and shrink back to normal size.

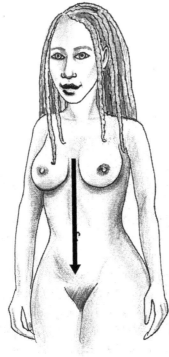

Energy flows from breasts/heart center to yoni.

Our breasts are often central during foreplay. Kissing, licking, and sucking the breasts and nipples arouses the sexual energy and makes our yoni juices flow.

Before we get deeper into our yoni, we must open the gate of the breasts. Through a daily practice of breast massage, you can:

- Naturally increase your estrogen levels (this helps manage and balance emotions as well as improve the skin).

- Activate your *qi* or life force energy. This will give you more vitality to carry out your daily tasks.

- Eliminate lumps or cysts in breasts. It may break up stagnant energy, which can develop into cancer.

- Increases sensitivity in breasts, making them more orgasmic.

- Can stop or shorten your menstrual cycle, make it less heavy, and reduces the pain. When we stimulate sexual energy in our breasts, we help transform blood into *qi*. Very similar to how nursing mothers don't menstruate. The energy goes into their breasts to make milk to nourish their child. We nourish ourselves with our loving *qi*.

- Make your yoni tighter, wetter, and more flexible.

- Inspire sensual self-love.

- Heal the heart chakra and nourish your ability to give and receive love.

★Breast massage can be easily done after showering or bathing. Try to do it twice a day for increased benefits. Breast massage is contraindicated for women with breast cancer. Any woman healing from cancer in the breasts can do an auric massage on her breasts, massaging the aura (energy) around her breasts without actually touching the breasts.

Let's first start with breast breathing to connect to our "bells of love."

Breast Breathing

- Sit up with your feet flat on the floor, your shirt off, and braless. You can also sit cross-legged on a cushion if you like.

- You are going to breathe up energy from the earth. In Taoism, the earth represents feminine or *yin* energy. Imagine that roots are coming down from your feet and going into the earth. Draw up energy from the earth, through the soles of your feet, up your legs and belly, all the way up to your breasts. Feel the nurturing energy of Mother Earth. Hold your breath for a few seconds and exhale it out. Repeat this several times, drawing in the energy from the earth to nurture your breasts.

- Next, we will breathe down energy from the heavens. In Taoism, the heavens represent masculine or *yang* energy. Connect to the heavens and feel the energy of enlightenment and conscious awareness. Breathe it down through your head, to your throat, upper chest, and then to your breasts. Hold the energy and breath in your breasts for a few seconds, and then exhale. Repeat this several times, drawing in the energy and light from the heavens into your breasts.

- Finally, you will breathe up energy from the earth into your breasts and hold. Without exhaling, take another sip of air breathing down energy from the heavens. Hold the breath now, feeling both energies mix in sacred union. Breathe out, feel your breast expand on the exhalation. Repeat twice more, feeling not only your breast expand but your heart radiating out love. You can imagine energy, the color of pink, radiating out from your breasts and magnetizing more love to you.

- Smile to your breasts! Love them no matter the shape or size.

Breast Massage Steps

- Just like breast breathing, you will begin sitting up either in a chair or on a soft cushion with no shirt or bra.

- You may have a soft ball or cloth rolled into a ball, putting gentle pressure on your clitoris if you like. I normally just stimulate my clitoris with my mind by gently pulsing my yoni. I imagine she is a flower and softly open and close the petals.

- Rub your hands together to prepare for the massage. This warms the hands and awakens the healing energy centers in your palms.

- Apply some oil to your breasts. This will make the massage easier and more sensual. Be sure to use a natural oil like coconut or almond. You may also mix it with an essential oil like rose or jasmine. Rose inspires self-love, and jasmine is an aphrodisiac that is known to improve mood and reduce depression. You can also use another scent you like.

- Place your hands on your breasts. Close your eyes and really feel the energy of your hands from inside your breasts.

- Contract your perineum to stimulate your sexual energy. It is located in the space between your yoni opening and anus. In Taoism, it is known as the Gate of Death and Life or *Hui-Yin*, the point where all the *yin* (feminine) energy converges. In

Tantra, it is the location of the root chakra. This is the same muscle you use to stop the flow of urine if you need to pee. As you contract and release several times, you will feel your yoni warm with sexual energy.

- First, you will massage in the direction of the earth. The earth is linked to feminine energy because it has deep reserves of water. Approximately 72% of our planet is water. Our bodies are also mostly made of water. Imagine that beneath your feet, there is a bubbling spring of water. You are going to draw this water up your legs to your yoni.

Earth Direction – Dispersing

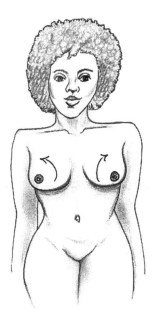

- Imagine a fountain of energy is coming up from your yoni. Take your hands, palms facing your yoni, and stroke it up from your yoni to the middle of your chest, around, and down the sides of your breasts. Continue to massage in this direction, up the middle and down the sides. Start in wide circles covering the entire breasts and gradually get closer to the nipple. Before reaching the nipples, begin again.

- Massaging your breasts in this direction will disperse stagnant energy in the breasts, which can cause lumps or cysts. It can make your breasts smaller and firmer. This direction also allows you to nurture yourself with loving feminine energy.

- Do this a minimum of 27 times and a maximum of 360. Taoists like to do things in multiples of nine; nine represents the completion of a cycle. So you could do 36, 45, 54, etc.

Heaven Direction – Gathering

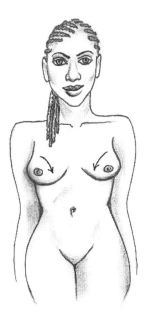

- For the heaven direction, imagine a beautiful bright star above your head. Your personal North Star, leading you to sexual freedom. Connect to the heavenly bliss of the cosmos.

- Breathe this energy down through your head as it blesses and lights up your master glands: the pineal, and pituitary. Feel the energy flow through your throat, down the center of your chest, up the sides, and back around again. You will massage your breasts in this direction, stroking down the center and up the sides, the reverse of the earth direction to gather more *qi* to you.

  This direction will make your breasts grow bigger and fuller, and it inspires self-confidence. (If you're working on decreasing lumps or cysts, I suggest focusing on the earth direction.)

- Repeat for the desired cycle of nine.

- Close this practice by placing your hands on your breasts and smiling to your bells of love. Notice how warm, sensual and supple they feel.

★You can also have a lover help you with the massage.

Enjoy your bells of love, ladies!!

Journal Reflection

1. What are the ways you would like to see your heart expand in love?

   _____

   _____

   _____

   _____

   _____

2. Describe the experience of sensually touching your breast. What did it feel like to nurture and heal your bells of love?

   _____

   _____

   _____

   _____

   _____

Day 6

Intention: Pleasure and heal your yoni through yoni breathing and massage.

Our wombs are the cradle of life and the key to our ability to manifest. In sacred sexuality, we have many more meaningful names for our sacred place other than vagina - which means sheath for a sword.

As mentioned, the female reproductive organ is called the yoni in Tantra, meaning "source of all life" and "sacred space." In Taoism, she is referred to as the "jade fountain," with jade being the most precious and sacred stone in China, and a fountain represents flowing waters of healing and nourishing *yin* energy. Yes, the good wetness!

Today, we will honor our own yoni or jade fountain with the same intentions of the ancients who worshipped her as the symbol of the Goddess and the life-giving principle of the divine. We will begin with yoni breathing.

Yoni Breathing

- You can sit up with your feet on the floor or lay down. You may want some pillows behind your back to prop you up if you lay down.

- Make a triangle with your hands, allowing the tips of your thumbs and index fingers to touch. Place the triangle upside down on your womb, with your index fingers touching the middle of your pubic bone, thumbs under your belly button, and palms over your ovaries.

- You're going to breathe in deeply from the earth. Imagine this energy traveling from the soles of your feet and up your legs, just like in the breast breathing exercise, bringing nourishing energy into your yoni. Contract your yoni muscles holding in the breath for a few seconds and then exhale it out, and relax your yoni muscles. You can repeat this earth breath two or three times.

- Next, you will inhale energy down from the heavens through your crown chakra (top of head) all the way down into your yoni. You can imagine a white light moving down to fill your yoni. Feel her expand as you breathe in. Imagine the white light cleansing any blockages.

- Hold the breath, and while holding your breath, contract your yoni muscles. Hold for a few seconds and exhale out. Repeat two to three times.

- For the final round, without exhaling your first breath, draw energy up from the earth and down from the heavens. Feel earth and heaven energy mix in your jade fountain, creating balance. Exhale it out and feel the energy expanding across your womb, into your ovaries, pelvic floor, etc. You should start to feel orgasmic energy beginning to swirl inside your jade fountain.

Yoni Massage

After the yoni breathing, it's time to pleasure her with a massage! You can do this alone or ask a partner to help you. Massaging your yoni on a regular basis will also help to break up stagnant *qi* that leads to painful menses and reproductive ailments. It will also make her more sensitive to the flow of orgasmic energy.

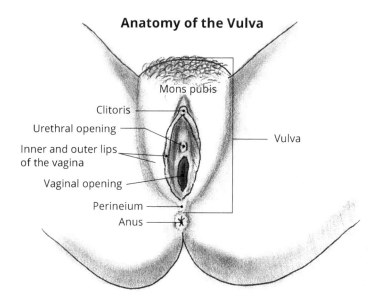

Anatomy of the Vulva

Mons pubis

Clitoris

Urethral opening

Inner and outer lips
of the vagina

Vaginal opening

Perineium

Anus

Vulva

- Rub your hands together to warm them and awaken the healing centers in the palm. Apply natural massage oil to your yoni. (I wouldn't recommend using any essential oil here because it will irritate the yoni if it gets inside.)

- Slowly and sensually, with intention, massage all around your vulva. Start with the pubis mound. Make sure you also massage the crease between your yoni and inner thighs; a lot of lymph nodes and blood vessels lie there. This will help prevent energy stagnation that leads to menstrual cramps and help your lymphatic system flush out toxins.

- Massage and lightly tap on the ovaries. A way to easily find the ovaries is by placing both your hands, side-to-side, palms facing down, on your womb. Have your fingertips touching the top of your pelvic bone, and around where the pinky fingers land should be the ovaries. You can feel around for them; they may feel like two eyeballs underneath the flesh.

- Massage the yoni lips, both inner and outer. Massage the opening to your yoni, which Taoists call the "jade gate" to increase the proper circulation of blood and life force energy.

- If it feels right (and you have time), massage the inside of the yoni. (Be sure your hands and fingernails are clean.) Allow the sexual energy to flow naturally. Release through the breath and mouth whatever sounds feel natural. Try releasing with the sounds "Ahhhhhh" or "Haaaaaaa" as they help clear the heart and bring the fire of the heart down to bring heat to the sexual waters of the yoni.

- If you desire, allow yourself to climax. Unlike men (if they ejaculate), women do not lose energy through orgasms; we gain energy!

Journal Reflection

1. How often do you touch your yoni? What was it like to explore your yoni through sensual massage?

2. What are some of your yoni's favorite ways to receive pleasure?

Day 7

Intention: Enjoy something that brings you pleasure and indulge in a Cleansing Goddess bath.

This is our last exercise for our Pleasure Week. Congrats, Goddess, on making it through the first week! I hope you had fun committing to carving out the time to complete these yummy exercises. Are you swimming in wetness yet? I hope your breasts and yoni are feeling really orgasmic!

Today you have two tasks I hope you enjoy completing:

1. **Take Yo' Pleasure!**

   Remember the list of 100 things that bring you pleasure? Go back to it, choose something from the list and allow yourself to enjoy it. It could be as simple as eating some Godiva chocolate, or as grandiose as booking a trip to Jamaica! You decide!

2. **Cleansing Goddess Bath!**

   I would like to introduce you to what will be a weekly ritual for us during our 30-day deep dive: a goddess bath. Spiritual bathing is thousands of years old and practiced by the ancients to remove negative energy, relieve stress, and bring in the positive energy desired.

   As vibrational beings, we collect and attract vibrations to us. Sometimes when we are feeling down, stressed, or unable to tap into our pleasure it is because our aura (spiritual body) has picked up the negative influences around us. One of the most effective ways to cleanse our vibration is by taking a spiritual bath. Water has long been recognized as a healing element. Every year people flood the shores of the beach to experience the relaxation one feels when at the ocean.

This is a simple bath inspired by the ocean.

Ingredients:

- 1 cup of natural sea salt or epsom salt
- ½ cup of apple cider vinegar
- 7-10 drops of essential oil of lavender (can get from health food store or online)
- 2 handfuls of white flower petals (buy a bouquet of flowers and remove some petals)

Lavender is good for relaxing the entire body, protecting your aura, activating the crown chakra, cleansing your energy meridians, and establishing emotional balance. It is also good for headaches, insomnia, pains, depression and brings mental alertness.

Incense: Sage, palo santo, rosemary, or frankincense.

Sage is an herb that comes from Native American culture and is a powerful cleansing and balancing agent. It awakens spiritual faculties and releases tensions stored in the body. Unfortunately, sage is now being endangered due to the commercialization of something that was once sacred. If you have sage, use it sparingly. It does not need to be burned every day. It is like taking an antibiotic and will remove everything energetically. If you use it, be sure to burn a sweet-smelling incense afterward to bring back the positive energy.

Palo santo is a good alternative to sage and cleanses negative energy while bringing in positive energy. Burning the herb rosemary helps to clear negative energy and is strongly connected to feminine energy. Frankincense aids in meditation, promotes peace, and relieves anxiety. Both of these are also good alternatives to sage or to support it.

Steps:

1. Run your bath water nice and hot.
2. Once half full, add the sea salt and vinegar. Both the salt and vinegar are cleansing spiritually and helps relax tired muscles.
3. Add the lavender oil to your water.
4. Sprinkle flower petals on top. They will bring sweet, healing energy.
5. As you are adding the ingredients, state your intentions into the water. Water picks up vibrations and the molecules will begin to rearrange themselves based on your energy (Google Dr. Masaru Emoto's water experiment). An example of an intention is: "May this bath cleanse me of all negative energy and open me to experience more pleasure and bliss etc."
6. Light your white and blue candles in the bathroom. White purifies your energy, while blue emits healing vibrations.
7. As you lay in the bath, allow your entire body to relax. You can meditate and massage your body with the saltwater asking the Spirit to cleanse you of any negative energy and allow the light of pure positive energy to come in.
8. Once you finish the bath, towel off and dress in comfortable clothing.
9. Spend the evening doing something you enjoy. You should sleep well.

Journal Reflection

1. How often do you take a bath as opposed to a shower? How did it feel to take a bath with intention?

   _____

   _____

   _____

   _____

   _____

2. Reflect on how this week went for you. Do you notice any changes in your overall mood and wellbeing as a result of connecting to your pleasure?

   _____

   _____

   _____

   _____

   _____

WEEK 2:

JUICY

Introduction

> *Juicy got 'em crazy, got 'em crazy...*
> *got 'em cold goin' mad."*
> **—Oaktown's 357**

Soft. Wet. Slippery. Flowing. Receptive. Sensitive. Dripping. Juicy!

When the natural tap of your wetness is turned on, it's sure to drive your lover out of their minds!

Yes, ladies, we've come to week 2, where our theme is JUICY! We focus this week on the characteristic of feminine energy that has to do with being like water. As women, our nature is *yin*, and water is a *yin* element. Our emotions ebb and flow like ocean tides. When we move and dance, our bodies undulate like the river.

Water is arguably the most powerful element on the earth. It nurtures and nourishes, makes nature grow lush and green. Water is life! To be a healthy and happy woman is to be a juicy woman on the outside and the inside. Being well lubricated is a sign of estrogen flowing properly and is key to great sex. So this week, we will be focusing on our yoni, the throne of juiciness! We will also learn some internal alchemy to turn on the faucet of our bliss.

Our yonis are delicate flowers and, without proper lubrication, they can get damaged. Vaginal dryness affects many women after menopause but also younger women who may feel disconnected sexually, stressed out, or have hormonal imbalances. When the yoni is dry, she becomes susceptible to illness and disease. Sexual intercourse becomes painful, often resulting in cuts and bruises.

A healthy yoni is a wet yoni. We become lubricated through glands found in the cervix. The fluid produced by these glands travels down the cervix through the vaginal canal. It helps remove dead cells in the yoni and keeps her naturally clean. This is why douching is unnecessary and actually harmful to the yoni as it removes healthy bacteria that live there. The vagina has a natural healing mechanism that can be helped along through a balanced diet full of fresh fruits, vegetables and drinking lots of water.

If I ever notice anything "off" with my yoni, I treat it internally by drinking a cup of warm water with a tablespoon of organic, raw, unfiltered apple cider vinegar three times a day. This will usually clear any unusual smells or discharge in three days. Apple cider vinegar helps to balance the PH levels in the vagina, which is the level of acidity or alkalinity. Vaginas are naturally more acidic. Apple cider vinegar also has many antiviral and antifungal properties. Of course, see a medical professional if you have serious symptoms that do not clear up on their own in a reasonable amount of time.

There are many natural ways to keep our yoni juicy and ensure highly pleasurable sex. When a woman is aroused, her lubrication is increased by the Bartholin's glands located at the opening of the vagina. However, if she does not engage in enough foreplay, is not relaxed, or does not feel safe, the well will run dry. One natural method we will use to keep our waters flowing this week is the jade egg or yoni egg. I shared with you in the introduction about buying my first egg. I've been using it for the past 11 years, and it is a powerful tool.

The practice of inserting an egg made of gemstones into the vagina is thousands of years old. It began in ancient China as a secret practice that only the Queen and concubines of the royal court were taught. The women who used it had great physical and spiritual health. They were able to become "immortal," keeping youthful, juicy, and tight sexual organs like that of a much younger woman.

The egg was used to tone the vagina and stimulate the sexual reflexology zones found in the vaginal canal. The egg also activates the root chakra or *qi* muscles to send sexual energy up into the higher spiritual centers. The egg is also perfectly safe inside the yoni and cannot go past the cervix, so don't worry; it won't get "lost" in there.

When beginning with this practice, it is suggested that one starts with the jade stone. Jade is the most prized stone of Chinese culture, symbolizing wealth, health, and longevity. Jade helps to bring emotional balance, peace, love, and harmony. It is healing to the kidneys (ruler of sexual energy) and the heart. It is also considered a dream stone, which helps you to "dream solve". You can place the egg inside your yoni when going to sleep at night with an intention to get insight into a problem from your dreams.

In the last decade or so, yoni egg use has become very popular, with women like actress Regina Hall speaking on late-night television about using them. There are also many yoni egg sellers online who dazzle you with all types of stones. What I have found is that majority of yoni egg sellers, and even women who claim to teach yoni egg use online, have no idea about the practices from which they derive. The use of the jade or yoni egg is an ancient Taoist practice. There are certain techniques and practices one must experience prior to initiating with the yoni egg. It is more complex than just inserting a crystal inside your vagina and doing Kegels. It is a spiritual and wellness practice.

Contrary to popular belief, you don't need a bunch of different stones or different shapes and sizes. There are only three main stones that I practice with, and for the most part, a medium egg will serve most women well. I have already shared about the power of jade. The two other types of crystals used for yoni eggs that are common with Taoist lineage practitioners are below.

1. **Rose Quartz:** This stone is like a bubble bath for the soul. It is considered the stone of love because it has a very feminine and romantic energy. It helps the heart to release resentment and heartache. It represents unconditional love, attraction, compassion, intimacy, love of beauty and art, etc.

2. **Obsidian:** A powerful cleanser that is actually not a crystal but formed from volcanic lava that cooled very quickly. It will shield you from negative energy and is a strong protection stone. It is like a mirror, exposing hidden parts of you: your patterns and things you need to see so you may let them go and evolve. It helps you to release negative attitudes, thoughts, etc. It can be very intense, and you must be willing to confront your issues.

There are other stones that people like to use for yoni eggs, such as red jasper, tiger's eye, bloodstone, clear quartz, smoky quartz, and others. Be sure that if you choose to work with a particular stone, that it is non-porous and doesn't have harmful metals that could leak inside your body. Look for sellers who offer eggs that are certified by the Gemological Institute of America (GIA), so you know the crystal is authentic. GIA has been the leading source of knowledge, standards, and education in gems and jewelry since 1931.

Along with the various healing and spiritual properties of these stones, wearing them inside the yoni makes her more sensitive, lubricated, and awakens deep pleasure. If lubrication is an issue for you, or you just want to keep it extra healthy and juicy, you may want to research different herbs. Below are some herbs that I like to use to keep me wet and in balance. They are beneficial not just for lubrication but also for the womb and overall wellness.

1. **Dong Quai** - This is one of my favorite herbs. It is famous in Chinese medicine, considered the "female ginseng." It balances estrogen levels and increases fertility. It has great vitamin and mineral content as it's rich in B12, folic acid, and biotin. It can help treat iron deficiency and anemia. *Dong quai* also reduces anxiety and promotes relaxation. I love to drink it as a tea or take it in honey-based syrup.

   Note: *Dong quai* is not to be used if you are on your menstrual cycle, are pregnant, or nursing. If you have been diagnosed with breast cancer, uterine fibroids, or endometriosis, please see a Chinese herbalist or doctor of Chinese medicine who can design a specific formula to help with these issues and refrain from using *dong quai*.

2. **Slippery Elm** – It comes from the bark of the slippery elm tree and has a wide range of uses. It helps to internally coat and soothe mucous membranes while also absorbing toxins. It is nutrient-rich, containing vitamin C, calcium, iron, magnesium, potassium, zinc, and B vitamins. Slippery elm will keep you slippery, baby!

3. **Nettles Leaf** – This herb is great for many things, including womb health. It boosts your immunity and is rich in B vitamins, vitamin K, protein, calcium, selenium, and zinc. It nourishes the fetus if you're pregnant and helps nursing mothers lactate. It will decrease menstrual cramps and bloating. It is a very nourishing and nutritive herb that should be a part of every woman's personal apothecary.

4. **Red Raspberry Leaf** – A herb highly recommended during pregnancy for its ability to tone the uterus and reproductive organs. It brings hormonal balance, is a blood tonic rich in vitamins A, B, C, and E, as well as iron, potassium, manganese, and zinc.

5. **Maca Root** – An ancient Peruvian herb that has gained recent popularity, maca has many nutrients such as vitamins B, C, and E. It also packs calcium, zinc, iron, and amino acids. It is a libido enhancer and increases fertility and endurance. Maca balances the hormones, relieves menstrual issues and menopause. It is known to relieve cramps, body pains, anxiety, depression and, mood swings. Note: Do not take maca root if you are pregnant or breastfeeding.

6. **Dandelion Root** - One of the key factors in heavy bleeding and blood clots during menstruation is our bodies overly producing estrogen or estrogen dominance. When our liver is congested, it becomes hard for it to metabolize our estrogen. To help detoxify the liver, drink dandelion root tea.

7. **Mugwort** - Mugwort is another great herb to have. This herb can be used as a tea and also great in yoni steams. As a tea, it acts as a liver tonic. It also helps promote circulation, calms nerves, and relieves anxiety. It stimulates menstruation for late periods and regulates the menstrual cycle. Spiritualists also use mugwort to promote vivid dreams and astral projection.

8. **Damiana** - Got a lover coming over or ready for some self-pleasure? Invite ya girl damiana to the party! This herb is a natural aphrodisiac that increases circulation and sensitivity to female organs. It also improves mental function and mood, helps depression, treats headaches, and helps with stress relief.

All these herbs are rich in vitamins and minerals that nourish the body and help to balance the hormones naturally. Hormonal imbalance is the main cause behind vaginal dryness. Also, eat foods rich in essential fatty acids like salmon, tuna, and sunflower seeds. You can also take Omega-3 supplements; make sure they are high quality. Avoid consuming excess alcohol and caffeine, both of which are diuretics that dry you out. Stay hydrated by drinking lots of water. I also love to drink natural coconut water as it contains a lot of electrolytes.

Enjoy the activities this week, get to know your yoni well! She is your personal pleasure palace!

Items Needed for Juicy Week

- Drilled yoni egg
- Non-minty dental floss or clean string
- Massage oil
- 4–5 oranges
- Honey

Week 2: Juicy

Quote for the week:

Candy rain
Comin' down
Taste you in my mind
And spread you all around

Here I am
Oh, this love's for you
Hey, baby
Sweet as honey dew…

Juicy fruit (You're so)
Juicy (Juicy)
Juicy fruit (Yeah…hey…hey…hey…hey)
Juicy…
—Mtume

Day 8

Intention: Connect with early memories and associations to your yoni.

Hey, hey, you juicy woman! You know you got that good stuff, right? This week's exercises are going to allow you to explore just how good it is. It doesn't matter if you've had twenty partners or one. You could be sexing every day or not sexing at all. You are going to own your goodness and get your waters flowing, all for you!

Journal Reflection

This week we will begin with a reflection about our jade fountain.

1. How many different words for vagina can you think of? Make a list! Think of everything from the cute, to the obscure, to the raunchy. Try making up a few of your own! If you don't have one already, create a secret sexy name for your yoni. Have fun, and be playful.

_____

_____

_____

_____

_____

2. I want you to think back to when you were a little girl. What was one of the first experiences you had with your yoni? What were the messages you received from your family about her? (If early experiences include abuse and trauma, please be gentle with yourself. I also suggest using the healing sounds to release any pent-up emotions this may stir up for you. See the Introduction in Pleasure week.)

_____

_____

_____

_____

_____

Day 9

Intention: Look at your yoni with new eyes and express your love for her.

Today, we are going to go further into exploring our jade fountain. Too often, many of us never take time to gaze at our goddess. We allow others, like our doctors and our lovers, full access but hardly look "down there" unless we are looking to see if something is "wrong." Only looking at our yoni when something is awry can leave a negative imprint. Today we will look at our yoni with soft loving eyes. If we want others to look at our yonis with love and respect, we must as well.

Yoni Gazing and Love Letter

- Get out a handheld mirror (or you can even use the camera on your phone) and look at your yoni.

- What do you notice about her? The shape, colors, etc.

- Each yoni is different (some traditions note nine different types). Notice three things that you like about your yoni.

- Once you finish your yoni gazing, take some paper and begin writing a love letter to her.

- Imagine that you are your own lover; how would you want someone to talk to your yoni? What would your ideal lover say to her? How would they honor you and your sacred space? If you can radiate this within, you will attract this.

- Once you finish, read the letter out loud.

- End this practice with a nice yoni massage; try warming the oil.

Journal Reflection

Make a yoni picture! You can draw, sketch, paint, or make a visual picture with words of your yoni. Try printing images from the internet or cutting out images from magazines that represent your yoni and gluing it in your journal.

Day 10

Intention: Create a juicy aura and more radiance through the Inner Smile meditation.

Have you ever been in the presence of someone who is absolutely radiant? Perhaps imagine a mother with her newborn baby, couples on their honeymoon, or you on vacation in your favorite place. One of my Tao-Tantra teachers, Minke de Vos, says that "Radiance is the best protection". When we are vibrating high and feeling good, we create a protective shield that bounces negativity off us.

We all have energy bodies or auras that extend beyond our physical bodies. Some psychics can even see this energy that projects from the body. We will create a juicy radiant aura through a Taoist meditation called the Inner Smile.

Inner Smile

Did you know that smiling makes the body more alkaline and boosts the immune system? Someone giving you negative energy through a nasty look can actually lower your immune system. When we smile to ourselves with unconditional love, we raise our vibration. Through the alchemy of this meditation practice, we will transform negative energy and stress into self-acceptance and radiance. Follow the instructions below.

Inner Smile Meditation Instructions

1. Begin the meditation by closing your eyes and doing some deep breathing for a few moments until you are relaxed. You may want to play some light meditation music or do it in silence.

2. Once relaxed, imagine a person you love standing in front of you. Be sure it's a person with whom you have no tension around loving. See this person smiling at you. You can also imagine the sun shining its unconditional loving rays on you.

3. Visualize this unconditional loving energy pouring toward you as warm golden light. In Taoism, gold represents that which doesn't tarnish: the pure essence of you. Feel the warmth of this energy touch your face. Draw the energy into your third eye chakra – the midpoint between your eyebrows. Allow your mouth to curve into a smile. Feel the smile spread warm energy into your head, activating the energy centers that lie there. Imagine it glowing with a soft and warm light.

4. Allow the light to spread to your face, relaxing your facial muscles, and then move down to your throat, healing any blockage there that prevents you from speaking your truth.

5. When you're ready to move on, see it travel to your heart. Allow the light to stay in your heart as long as you need it to, to send warmth, and cleanse out any heartbreak or resentment. Imagine your heart and chest glowing golden pink with the energy of unconditional self-love.

6. Spiral the energy down into your stomach, releasing any tension or anxiety there until you reach your womb. Feel the golden pink light warm your yoni, filling her with a loving energy. Ask for the light to turn on the natural juiciness of your yoni.

7. From here, feel free to play with the light, allowing it to go into any part of the body that needs healing or release. Tell every cell in your body, "I love you." See your entire body glowing with a golden pink aura of pure radiance.

8. When you finish, imagine the light crystalizing into a tiny pearl that you store behind your navel.

Journal Reflection

1. Describe your experience doing the Inner Smile meditation. Were you able to connect to the energy of unconditional love? Is accepting unconditional love easy or hard for you? Do you have an easier time giving love or receiving love?

_____

_____

_____

_____

_____

2. As you are walking about the world, do you smile, or is your face an immovable mask? Do you notice your mood raising just by lifting the corners of your mouth? What kind of aura do you think you walk around with?

_____

_____

_____

_____

_____

Day 11

Intention: Open up your energy channels to experience the juiciness of flowing *qi*.

Yesterday we focused on boosting our radiance through the Inner Smile meditation. Today we will tune into the subtle flow of life force energy that circulates around our body to awaken our energy even more.

Thousands of years ago, Taoist masters intuited that there was an underlying energy animating the universe. This life force energy called *qi* is what determines how healthy and vital a person is. Within the body, it was discovered that *qi* moved through certain energy channels. As they began to meditate and study, they observed one particularly strong route that *qi* flowed through.

This route began at the navel, flowed down to the perineum, up the back, to the top of the head, down the front of the body, and back to the navel. They called this pathway the Microcosmic Orbit.

While everyone has this orbit, not everyone's is fully activated. Opening up the Microcosmic Orbit is key to raising sexual energy into the higher spiritual centers, having full-body orgasms, and engaging in multi-orgasmic love-making with a partner. It is also believed that circulating energy in the Microcosmic Orbit can heal insomnia, headaches, hot flashes, high blood pressure and open one up to spiritual enlightenment and psychic powers.

Imagine this orbit in our body as a piping system in a house. When a pipe gets clogged, water will move sluggishly through it or not at all. As a result, our sink gets stopped up because the water cannot move freely. The same thing happens in our body; our channels or meridians get clogged, and energy stagnates. We must work to clear out the blockages and open the pathways, and the Microcosmic Orbit meditation will help you do this.

You will be breathing the energy up points along the spine. These points act as pumps, sending the energy up while also refining the energy as it rises to the crown. As the energy becomes refined, it also becomes purified. It feeds the higher spiritual centers and is then exhaled down the front to be integrated by the entire body.

Learning the practice of the Microcosmic Orbit is a foundational practice in the Taoist system and opens the doors to sexual transmutation. The juice, aka *qi*, you circulate will nourish your cells to keep you healthy and vibrant.

Prior to the meditation, doing some movements to loosen the spine, like the cat-cow yoga pose, are particularly helpful. Read the instructions below about opening the orbit. At first, you may be relying primarily on your imagination to sense the orbit; then, with time, you will be able to sense the flow of energy wrapping around your body. It is a Taoist saying that "the *qi* (energy) follows the *yi (thought)*" – where intention or thought goes, energy flows…

Steps to Opening the Orbit

1. Sit in a chair or upright on the edge of your bed. Make sure your feet are flat on the floor. It's nice to do this barefoot to connect to the energy of the earth. There is a point on the soles of our feet called the Bubbling Spring or Kidney 1. This point is found under the big toe mound. It activates our kidney meridian. Massaging this point is a great way to balance and

enliven sexual energy. It may be sore when you touch it. You can massage this point prior to doing this meditation.

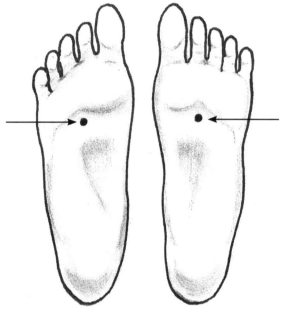

Bubbling Spring point

2. Breathe for a few minutes, feeling your energy roots going down into the earth from the Bubbling Spring point. Place the tip of your tongue on the roof of your mouth, right behind the teeth on the gum line. There are two channels of energy that begin and end in your mouth: the *yin*, or Conception Vessel, which runs up the front of the body, and the *yang*, or Governing Vessel, which runs up the back. When you place your tongue behind the teeth, you connect these two channels into one circuit of energy, masculine and feminine *qi* uniting with each other. You might even feel electricity or little sparks when you do it. (This is why we enjoy kissing so much: four circuits of energy meeting!)

3. Bring your awareness to your navel. Expand your belly with the inhale and gently contract it with the exhale. Feel your breath expand to include your yoni.

4. Next, focus on your perineum, the most *yin* or feminine point in your body. It is located between your yoni and anus. To activate this area squeeze your pelvic floor muscles. The way to feel this muscle is to contract as if you are trying to stop yourself from urinating. Imagine a golden ball of light radiating there at your perineum. Breathe into this ball of light for a few moments. On the inhale, gently contract it and release on the exhale. You may feel the subtle tingle of sexual energy.

5. Then inhale and imagine this ball of light traveling from the perineum up to your coccyx/tailbone where the sacral pump is. Leave it there, holding your breath for a few seconds. Then exhale and bring it back down to the perineum. Do this several times until you begin to feel a connection between your breath, intention, and the energy. Relax.

6. Inhale again, imagining the ball glowing in your perineum, and breathe it up past the coccyx to stop this time at the door of life/meng mein point. This point is located between your two kidneys and opposite your belly button. Hold it for a few moments and exhale it back to your perineum. Repeat two more times. Relax.

7. Continue this pattern of breathing into the perineum, imagining the golden ball and inhaling it up to the following points as shown in the picture:

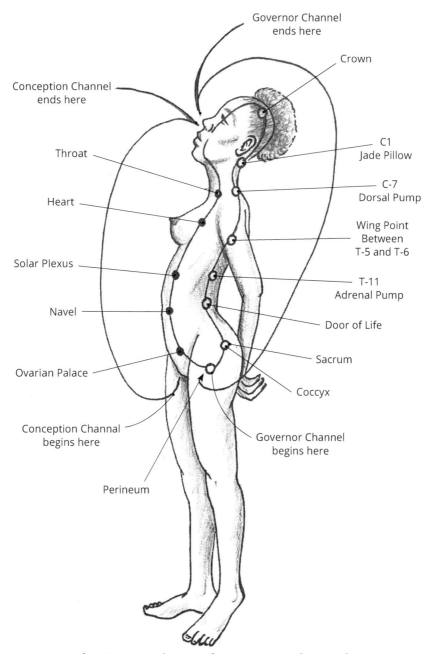

**The Conception and Governor Channels
and the Stations of the Microcosmic Orbit**

- T-11, Adrenal Pump (Across from your solar plexus)
- T5/6, Wing Point (Between your shoulder blades, across from your heart)
- C7, Dorsal Pump (Base of your neck where the large bone sticks out. Also called the "Great Hammer")
- C1, Jade Pillow (Bottom of your skull)
- Crown (Top of your head)

8. This first half of points are along the *yang* or masculine energy channel. Because *yang* energy is associated with fire, it is also known as the fire channel. Be sure to keep the tip of the tongue on the roof of the mouth while doing this. Bring the ball of energy down to your third eye and to the palate where the Governing Vessel ends.

9. Once the golden ball reaches your head, you are going to visualize it coming down the front of the body or *yin* channel as you exhale. You may feel it falling down like a waterfall. Breathe down through the following points:
   - Throat Center
   - Heart Center
   - Solar Plexus
   - Navel Center
   - Ovarian Palace
   - Perineum

10. If the points become too technical or confusing to you, you can just imagine the golden ball being inhaled from your perineum, up your back, over your head, then being exhaled down through the front of your body, back to your perineum. You can imagine

the energy falling like a waterfall down your front since this is the feminine channel. Be sure to keep the tip of your tongue on the roof of your mouth; this is what connects the *yin* and *yang* channels of your body and ensures the energy is moving properly.

11. You can actually reverse the flow of energy as well, breathing up the water or *yin* channel in the front of the body and down the fire or *yang* channel in the back of the body. Many women actually feel the Microcosmic Orbit more when breathing in this direction. Breathing in the water direction is helpful for cooling hot flashes for women during menopause. It also increases feelings and sensitivity because it passes the organs. When you bring it up the fire channel through the spine, it increases awareness. It helps to protect our energy and contain it. Experiment with both directions and notice any difference.

12. While doing this practice, you may feel a sense of peace, electricity flowing, or you may feel nothing at all. It is fine whatever you feel; do the mediation with the intention of being able to open up this pathway of *qi* within your body.

13. Try to circulate your energy in the orbit three or four times in each direction. When you finish the practice, store it behind your navel by imagining a golden light. Circulate this light nine times counterclockwise, getting bigger and bigger, then reverse it nine times clockwise, getting smaller until it is a golden pearl behind your navel. This is a safe place to store sexual energy for later access.

Journal Reflection

1. Were you able to sense the *qi* flowing through the Microcosmic Orbit? Which direction were you able to connect more with, breathing up the *yin* channel or up the *yang* channel?

_____

_____

_____

_____

_____

2. Describe any feelings or sensations you experienced during this meditation.

_____

_____

_____

_____

_____

Day 12

Intention: Initiate our yoni egg practice and connect our heart to our yoni.

Today we begin our work with the yoni egg. The ancient Egyptians, Greeks, and Romans used crystals and stones for healing for thousands of years. We will utilize these powerful tools to manifest our own healing.

As mentioned in the introduction, working with the egg on a regular basis can help eliminate and prevent menstrual disorders, fibroids, pelvic prolapse, and incontinence. It increases vaginal sensitivity and fluids, making sex more pleasurable while helping you gain control over the muscles in the vagina and pelvic floor. Yes, the egg will keep you tight and juicy!

We've already gone over the healing properties of stones like jade, rose quartz, and obsidian, so we will now program our yoni eggs with our own intentions.

First, you are going to clean and charge your egg, then complete the meditation below to form a connection with the crystal. Even if you've been using yoni eggs for a while, I suggest approaching this ceremony like it's your first time.

Part 1: Cleanse

1. Begin by making sure your egg is clean. You can do this by sterilizing it if the egg is new or needs to be cleaned thoroughly. Bring water to a boil in a pot. Place the egg in a container like a ceramic mug or bowl and pour the boiling water on the egg. (You do not need to boil the egg. Some stones like rose quartz

may crack.) Add sea salt to cleanse energetically and let your egg sit in the mixture for up to 30 mins.

2. After sterilizing, rinse your egg thoroughly with warm water. You can also clean your egg with a gentle cleanser like castile soap or diluted tea tree oil to kill any bacteria (be sure to rinse it thoroughly if you use tea tree oil because it will burn). You can also smudge the egg with sage.

3. To charge your egg, leave it out in the sunlight or moonlight and allow it to soak up solar and/or lunar energies.

4. Once cleansed and charged, loop a non-minty dental floss or clean string through your egg for easy removal. Use about 12-18 inches, string it through the hole and tie a knot.

Part 2: Meditation and Yoni Egg Ritual

1. While this exercise can be done on the bed, you may want to create a place on the floor using a yoga mat and pillows, blankets, etc., to make yourself comfortable. Begin by lying naked on your back. You can have your knees raised and bent with feet flat on the floor, or perhaps have your legs down and open in a diamond shape with the bottoms of your feet touching.

2. You can rest the yoni egg on your belly to warm it or have it somewhere nearby. Rub your hands together. Grab some oil and give yourself a nice long massage to your breasts, womb, ovaries, and yoni. This will bring heat, release stagnation, and bring the positive flow of *qi* to your reproductive organs.

3. Once you have finished the massage, take the yoni egg, place it in your left hand and place it over your heart. Place your right hand over your yoni. (If you are left-handed, then reverse it.) Breathe in and out, sending loving energy down from your heart to your yoni.

4. Visualize the green energy flowing from the egg to your heart and down to the yoni. Green is the color of the heart chakra and wood element. Ask your heart is there anything she needs to release through doing this practice. If she has something, try releasing it with the heart healing sound "HAAAAAAWWWW." Make the healing sound as many times as you need to feel balanced and peaceful.

5. Bring your egg to your mouth and speak your healing intention into the egg. What would you like her to help you do? Heal your heart? Attract more abundance? Create better boundaries? Fill you up with juiciness? Whatever it is you want, speak it to her.

6. When you feel you are ready, place the yoni egg at the entrance of your yoni. You can add saliva to the egg for natural lubrication. Ask your yoni for permission to begin this practice. When you feel she has given you permission, place the tip of the yoni egg into your yoni and breathe in. As you breathe in, squeeze the egg with your yoni muscles, and as you breathe out, relax and allow your yoni to open. You may want to breathe out using the sound "Ahhhhhhh" to help you relax even deeper. Apply gentle pressure to the egg and gently guide it in, continuing the breathing pattern until the egg is securely inside. Imagine your yoni sipping the egg up.

7. Once your egg is in, you can practice inhaling and squeezing the egg with your yoni (contract your muscles as if you're trying to hold your urine in) and breathing out and relaxing. As you do this, the egg is moving up and down your yoni, massaging the various reflexology zones that lie there. You can add the Microcosmic Orbit meditation to this practice to help move the energy up the back and down the front and vice versa.

8. You can also imagine your yoni canal divided into three parts (lower, middle, and upper) and practice isolating each part by squeezing each section separately. Some sections may be easier to isolate than others.

9. Enjoy this practice by having an attitude of play with it. Once you are finished, if using a drilled egg, you can use the string to remove it. If undrilled, you can squat and bear down to "lay your egg" once you are finished with your practice. (Some women get tense, which doesn't allow them to release the egg. If your egg doesn't come out immediately, just relax; maybe it has more work to do. It will exit when it is ready.)

10. You can cleanse your egg with natural soap and water and store it for later use.

★If you are menstruating, please visit the section in this book that features practices you can do while menstruating.

Journal Reflection

1. Reflect on the yoni egg ritual. What thoughts, emotions, and sensations did you experience during the yoni egg practice?

    _____

    _____

    _____

    _____

    _____

2. What intention did you set with your egg? Notice over time any special ways your egg helps you magically manifest it.

    _____

    _____

    _____

    _____

    _____

Day 13

Intention: Stimulate the reflexology zones in the vagina with the corresponding healing sounds and the yoni egg.

Today we are moving deeper into our yoni egg practice. The study of reflexology is thousands of years old. Ancient Taoists discovered that when certain parts of our body are stimulated, it activates other organs/ body parts as well. Reflexology is a way to bring healing to our major organs and glands.

The yoni, and *lingam* (Sanskrit word for penis, meaning "wand of light"), reflect each other's reflexology zones. When we have intercourse, we are naturally stimulating the entire body for increased health and well-being.

When we use the yoni egg, we also stimulate these same reflexology zones as we move the egg up and down our vaginal canal. When we combine moving the egg with the healing sounds, we create a very powerful and dynamic practice.

As women, we can hold trauma and wounded emotions in our jade fountain, which can hold us back from having self-love, deeper vaginal orgasms, and satisfying sex. Through working with the sounds, we will release any negative feelings trapped in our yoni.

★Even if you can't "feel" every zone as you move through them, use your imagination, and with time, you'll become more sensitive to the various areas and be able to isolate them. Your intention is powerful enough!

Reflexology with Yoni Egg and Healing Sounds Practice

GENITAL REFLEXOLOGY

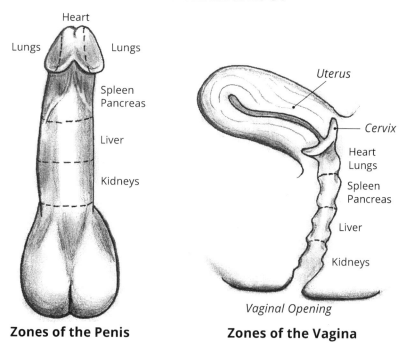

Zones of the Penis   **Zones of the Vagina**

- Sit or lay comfortably with legs open ready for practice.
- Take a few deep yoni breaths to open up. You can also do a breast massage and yoni massage.
- Sip the egg in using the breath like in yesterday's practice.

1. Focus on the kidney zone in the yoni. Put your intention there and squeeze the egg in that area with your vaginal muscles. Breathe in and squeeze, and then breathe out with the sound, "TCHOOO." Relax your muscles. Let go of any fear or

loneliness with the healing sound. Imagine dark or smoky energy leaving the yoni and going into the earth. Imagine calm blue light filling in the yoni.

2. Sip your egg up into the liver zone. Inhale, squeeze the egg, release, and breathe out with the sound "SHHHH." Release any anger, jealousy, and resentment into the earth. Imagine your yoni being filled with the green light of kindness and hope.

3. Suck your egg deeper into the spleen zone. Breathe in, and squeeze. Exhale and release on the sound "WHOOO." Let go of any worry or anxiety into the earth. Breathe in the yellow light of groundedness and mental stability.

4. Sip your egg up into the lung zone. Breathe in and squeeze, release and breathe out on the sound "SSSSS." Release any grief, sadness, or depression. Fill up with the white light of courage and inspiration.

5. Breathe your egg deeper towards the cervix. This is the heart zone. (This is why deep thrusting during sex is very bonding, opening, and can be scary or even painful. The area around our cervix is connected to our heart.) Breathe in and release on the sound "HAAAAWW." Release any hatred, shame, or bitterness. Breathe in the red light of joy, compassion, and happiness.

6. Breathe in and breathe out with the sound of "HEEEE." Let go of any energy that doesn't belong to you and anything left that you need to release.

7. You can do the Inner Smile Meditation to close. Imagine the warm golden light glowing in your yoni, filled with all the positive virtues you are cultivating. With the negative energy transmuted, imagine what you would like to manifest in your life with your healed feminine energy.

8. Remove your egg by pulling it out by the string. Wash your egg and cleanse with a sea salt mixture to purify the negative energy released.

Journal Reflection

Describe your experience releasing with the healing sounds and sexual reflexology? Reflect on what emotions, situations, etc., that you are choosing to let go of.

_____

_____

_____

_____

_____

_____

_____

_____

_____

Day 14

Intention: Sweeten your aura with an orange and honey bath.

For our final exercise this week, we are going to have a juicy bath. Here's what you need:

- 4–5 oranges
- Honey

Oranges are often presented as offerings to the Yoruba Goddess of healing, love, and fertility, Oshun. Honey is also sacred to Oshun as she is said to be as sweet as honey. To help sweeten our aura, we are going to bathe with oranges and honey.

Orange Honey Bath

- Take out oranges. Cut them into four pieces and place them into a large bowl. Taste the honey, then drizzle over the oranges.
- Prepare to take a shower, having the bowl of oranges nearby.
- You can light a candle and burn incense. Yellow candle and sandalwood incense is recommended.
- Shower as usual, focus on cleansing negative energy. You can also use healing sounds in the shower, seeing the negative energy slosh off your body and down the drain.
- Once you finish showering, take the orange slices and begin rubbing them all over your body.
- Recite affirmations, intentions, and prayers as you cleanse.

Here are some affirmations you can use.

1. I love and accept myself.

2. I let go of people who do not have my best interests at heart.

3. My yoni is a sacred temple of pleasure. I allow myself to experience pleasure now.

4. I am worthy of a juicy life that overflows with love and joy.

5. I open to receive more bliss, love, and abundance than I ever dreamed possible.

   - Once you have finished, rinse all excess orange pieces from your body in lukewarm shower water (DO NOT USE SOAP).

   - Allow your body to air dry. You can waft incense around your body.

Journal Reflection

1. Reflect on your juiciness. How juicy did you feel at the beginning of the week, and how juicy do you feel now?

_____

_____

_____

_____

_____

2. Write a poem in honor of your queen of succulence. Allow your yoni to inspire you!

_____

_____

_____

_____

_____

WEEK 3:

SEXY

Introduction

> *"Sex is the root, eroticism is the stem,*
> *and love is the flower."*
> **—Octavio Paz**

Sexual energy is the foundation of life. It is the creative energy that all life springs from. It is the union of egg and sperm through sexual intercourse that produces a child. Without sex, there is no life. This is why the ancients studied sexuality as a pathway to connecting to Spirit. The Spirit that flows through all life as people, trees, flowers, the sun, the moon, bees, and animals is creative sexual energy. If sex is so vital to life, why are we so ashamed of it? Why do we hide it, bury it, squelch it and shame each other for it? Because it is so powerful.

Most people are not awakened enough to fully handle the force of sexual energy, so it becomes restricted to lower-level pleasures like "busting a nut" or "getting off." In our current Western society, on one hand, we are sexually phobic: scared of anything overtly sexual, especially when it comes to the bodies of women. On the other hand, we are overwrought with sexual perversions, as evidenced through addictions to porn. Statistics state that 28,000 people are viewing porn every second. Addiction to pornography leaves people with a skewed view of sex that is completely divorced of love. Most often, pornography is filmed through the gaze of the male, with the women cast as hyper-sexualized objects with whom the man can "beat it up." Many women also feel trapped between the dichotomy of being either a virgin who is "pure" with no sexual desires or a whore who is sex-crazed. The modern world doesn't allow women to embrace the parts of themselves that are deeply spiritual and also deeply sexual.

This week as we focus on bringing out our inner sexy, we will be making a direct connection between that which allows life on this planet to continue and Spirit. We will do this by further awakening the flow of sexual energy in our own bodies.

In the Taoist tradition, sexual energy is considered to be the "water of life." It nourishes the totality of who we are: body, mind, and spirit. In the same way that when you water a garden, it grows lush and full, when we nurture ourselves with sexual energy, we too are healthier, happier, look younger, and are more creative. In Taoist theory, sexual energy called essence or *jing* represents the principal energy we are all born with in abundance. *Jing* is needed to carry out all functions of our body. As *jing* interacts with our vital organs, it becomes *qi*, life force energy. *Qi* is the energy that animates all life in the entire universe. It causes the planets to revolve, atoms to move, and is the force that allows the seed to grow into a tree. From *qi,* the energy is then transformed into *shen* or spiritual energy. The spiritual development path used by the Taoists focuses on raising the *jing* or sexual energy into *qi* so that it can nourish and revitalize our organs and then transform it into *shen* so

Taoist View of Women's Energy

Shen

Spiritual Energy

Qi

Life Force

Jing

Principle Energy

Transformation of Principal Energy (Jing) into Life Force (Qi) and Spiritual Energy (Shen)

that one can awaken spiritually. There is a direct link with cultivating sexual energy that leads to having a healthier body and a spiritually connected existence.

Jing is produced in our sexual organs (ovaries for women and testicles for men) and is the only energy that can be multiplied or increased. When we are young, we have lots of *jing* and use it freely, however as we get older and more stressed by life, around the age of twenty-four, the energy tends to be taxed and can become negative. Anger, worry, fear, and other detrimental emotions, plus increased sexual activity as we get older, eats up our good *jing qi*, leaving us feeling depleted. Through deliberately cultivating your principal sexual energy, you can conserve or restore what you've lost, which will result in you having more *qi*. As we recycle our sexual energy, we will be revitalized.

When sexual energy is flowing abundantly, it repairs hormonal dysfunctions, reduces cholesterol, and decreases blood pressure. The stimulation of sex glands enhances the hormones secreted by the other major endocrine glands: adrenal, thymus, thyroid, pituitary, and pineal. It stimulates growth hormones which helps slow aging. The people in ancient China who were able to master these sexual cultivation techniques were called immortal for a reason. As the women aged, they maintained the sexual organs, vitality, and appearance of someone much younger.

When our sexual energy is flowing properly, it has a positive effect on our emotions as well. You know when you've had some good, lip-smacking, orgasmic sex; the next day, you are happy, carefree, and energized. Imagine living every day like that? Not necessarily because somebody is "hitting it right" (though yes, we all deserve amazing sex) but because you've learned how to tap into your own inner fountain of youth. People with a healthy flow of *jing qi* have a warmth about them, a glow, and vitality, no matter their age. The key to maintaining an abundant flow of sexual energy is to spend time nourishing, cultivating, and storing it and being as stress-free as possible. Stress and negative emotions drain our life force.

The exercises this week will help you learn how to circulate, store, and recycle your *jing qi*. Mastering these techniques will increase your sexual energy (get ready), help you maintain womb health, alleviate problems during your moon cycle, foster more creativity, spark more vitality, and connect you with your spirit (*shen*).

This is truly being sexy: having a healthy flow of energy that keeps us joyous, blissful, and radiant.

Items Needed for Sexy Week

- Drilled yoni egg
- Additional yoni egg for weight lifting (if your yoni egg came in a small bag, you could use that or another small object)
- Yellow and pink flowers (needed at end of the week)
- Sweet-smelling essential oils like rose, geranium, orange, sandalwood, or jasmine, etc.
- Honey
- Yellow and pink candles
- Sweet-smelling incense (sandalwood or rose recommended)

Week 3: Sexy

Quote for the week:

The secret to sexuality is the absence of guilt. Sexual energy is the primal and creative energy of the Universe. Sexual desire is sacred. Bliss, carefreeness, and playfulness are the essence of sex.

—**Deepak Chopra**

Day 15

Intention: Create your perfect sexual fantasy.

To launch week three of our sensual deep dive, let's get ready to turn up the heat!

How do you feel when you are aroused? You get hot. Your temperature rises. Your pulse starts to quicken. Things seem to move in slow motion as if you are dancing in honey. Your entire body becomes super sensitive, and even a look from your beloved is enough to send shivers down your spine. You feel opened and surrendered. Amazing right? Well, that rush that you feel when aroused is the *jing qi* heating up and moving through your body. Before we learn to circulate this sacred primordial energy for our healing, let's heat up by creating our own perfect sexual fantasy!

I want you to imagine that you are an author. You are going to write a short story that embodies all the things you love about sexual intimacy. Forget played-out porn shot through a male gaze; you are going to create your own perfect sexual fantasy! Yours. Not your girlfriend's. Not your mama's. Not your partner's, YOURS. You get to cast yourself as the main character.

Here's what I'd like you to do:

- Choose a juicy setting (a moonlit beach, a riverbed in Jamaica, a subway car, a five-star hotel, etc.)

- Create your lover (it could be someone you're in a relationship with, a superstar or someone forged from the fabric of your imagination). What are they wearing? How do they talk to you? How do they touch your body?

- Embody your sexual goddess! Your sexual avatar is you at your best. What are you doing? How are you behaving, talking, making love, etc.? Allow yourself to behave without guilt or shame.

- Make sure your story has a beginning, middle, and end. Our best sexual fantasies allow for a build-up which makes the orgasmic release even more powerful. Don't skimp on the foreplay!

- Once you have your story, I want you to read it to yourself, slowly. As you read, close your eyes and imagine what you've read. See it in high definition!

The mind does not know the difference between what is imagined and what is real. It will fire off the same brain signals and physical responses as if it is actually happening. Your fantasy should make your temperature rise, your juices flow, and your sexual energy runneth over. If it doesn't, then you need to go back and pump it up.

Once you have it written to your liking, keep it somewhere safe and read it when you need a picker-upper. If possible, try to make it happen!

Journal Reflection

Was it easy to create your perfect sexual fantasy? Do you find it difficult or easy to allow your imagination to flow?

_____

_____

_____

_____

_____

_____

_____

_____

_____

_____

Day 16

Intention: Awaken sexual energy through sending love to the kidneys.

Today we are going to focus on the kidneys, the most powerful reservoir of *jing* in our bodies. As we spoke about before, *jing* is our sexual essence. We are born with a certain amount of *jing*; it carries our genetic blueprint and DNA within it (even the way the DNA spiral around one another is symbolic of making love). We need *jing* to live healthily, be strong and resilient. It creates and sustains the body's physical form.

When we are stressed or suffer from illness, our bodies will leak *jing*, and this *jing* is not replenished unless we adopt certain practices to restore it. Also, when we have weak *jing* or leaking *jing*, we will be more susceptible to disease and aging. Certain activities like meditation, *qi gong*, dietary changes, and consumption of certain herbs can all help restore *jing*. While we will focus on meditative practices and *qi gong* to restore *jing* here, it is also recommended that you see an herbalist or doctor of the Chinese medical arts if you'd like to further ascertain what is fully needed to replenish your *jing*.

The kidneys not only house the *jing* but are also considered to be the battery of the body. The health of all the other organs is dependent upon the proper functioning of the kidneys. As the governor of sexual energy, it affects fertility in women, ensuring the menstrual cycle is regular and assists the uterus with proper conception. In men, it helps achieve and maintain erections. When it is weak in men, they will suffer from erectile dysfunction and premature ejaculations. Weak kidney energy in women will cause frigidity, infertility, and a disconnection from sex. When the fire of the kidneys or kidney *yang* is healthy, there will be a strong desire for sex and a healthy libido. Bringing healing energy to the kidneys will also help release fear: a major blockage to freeing sexual energy.

To help maintain kidney health and help restore *jing*, we must give love to our kidneys on a regular basis. There are simple and powerful ways to do this. We will love our kidneys through massage, kidney breathing, and kidney packing.

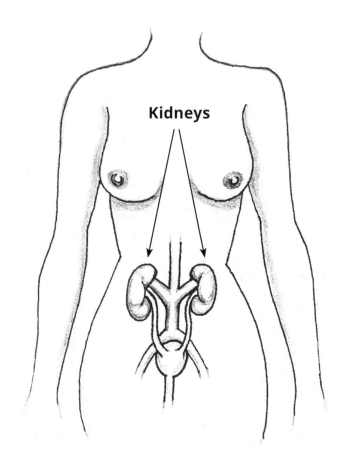

Part 1: Warming the Kidneys & Massage

This is a great practice to do first thing in the morning to energize you. It is also great to do during the winter, when kidney energy tends to be weak. *Jing* is considered to be solid and dense like ice, while *qi* is like water, able to move through everything, and *shen* is like a mist that envelops all. To assist the "ice" of the kidneys melting so energy can flow properly, we can warm up our kidneys.

1. Sit with your knees bent on your heels in a kneeling position. If your knees hurt in this position, you can also sit with your legs crossed. Rub your hands together to warm them.
2. Lean forward with your back curved, so your lower back is exposed.
3. Place your left hand over your left kidney and your right hand over your right kidney and rub them in a circular direction. Do this 90 times.
4. You should feel warm and energized afterward.

Ear Massage

You can also massage your ears to connect to the kidneys. If you look at your ears, they are shaped like kidneys, so you can enliven them and arouse sexual energy through massaging them. There are even schools of acupuncture that only needle on the ears as they contain reflexology points for the whole body. Sexually, when someone kisses or licks our ears, it is often stimulating and feels good. Give yourself an ear massage for about one minute. Feel the sensual energy awaken.

Massage Bubbling Spring

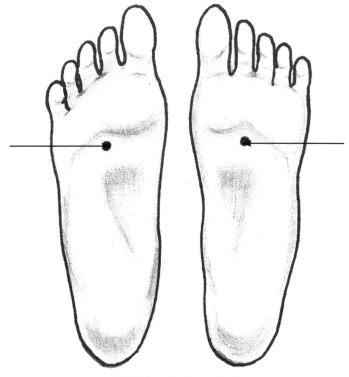

Bubbling Spring point

We discussed Kidney 1 or the Bubbling Spring point in last week's Microcosmic Orbit meditation practice. When we massage this point, we awaken and unblock the kidney energy. Find your Bubbling Spring point; once again, it may feel sore when you press into it. Give yourself a good massage over that point on both feet. You can use both hands.

Once you massage for a couple of minutes, sit wide-legged. You are then going to slap the Bubbling Spring point on your feet with each hand simultaneously and draw the energy up the inner legs, thighs, and into the groin. Here you are drawing energy up through the *yin* channel on the inside of the legs. Do this nine times.

Part 2: Kidney Breathing

As kidneys are the battery of the body, when you breathe into them, you charge them up. This is also a great exercise to do right before, during, or after your menstrual cycle. It can help ease lower back pain. Doing the kidney breathing will also open up the meng mein point, located midway between the kidneys. This point is considered to be the door of life where uncorrupted *qi* flows in. When this is open, we feel connected to Source Energy and receive the inherited gifts from our ancestors.

1. Sit with your legs bent on your heels again or cross-legged. Round your back and bend forward as you did with the kidney warming exercise, this time with your arms stretched out, resting on the floor in front of you.

2. You are going to breathe into the kidneys. Feel them expand on the breath and imagine them puffing up. Exhale.

3. Breathe into them nine times and on the ninth time, imagine wrapping them in a calm, blue, peaceful energy.

4. Smile to them and internally say peace three times.

5. Exhale.

Part 3: Kidney Packing

We are now going to nourish the kidneys even more by packing them with energy, utilizing a little bit of reflexology. Through "packing" or holding the breath, we intensify the energy and concentrate it wherever we want it to go.

1. You are going to take three sips of air. On the first sip of air, pull up the left side of your anus, which simultaneously stimulates the left kidney.
2. On the second sip of air, pull up or squeeze the right side of the anus and send the energy to the right kidney.
3. On the third sip of air, contract the center of the anus and send the energy to both kidneys.
4. Hold the breath for ten seconds or so, spiraling blue energy around the kidneys.
5. Exhale and imagine the blue energy going into the earth.

Notice how your energy feels now and throughout the day with your kidneys awakened and revitalized.

Journal Reflection

1. Describe any sensations you felt during the massages, kidney warming, packing, and breathing exercises. Did it arouse any sexual energy within you?

_____

_____

_____

_____

_____

2. Fear is the negative emotion of the kidneys. How fearful do you feel on a regular basis? What are some of the biggest fears you have that you are ready to let go of? How can you begin stepping out of your fear?

_____

_____

_____

_____

_____

Day 17

Intention: Move sexual energy up the spine through pelvic rocking with your yoni egg.

For the first yoni egg exercise this week, we are going to practice rocking our pelvis while squeezing our egg. This movement will help move the sexual energy up the spine and into our higher spiritual centers. By tugging on the string, we also add more resistance to the egg, making our yoni muscles more toned.

Rock Steady Yoni Eggercise

1. Lay down with your back against the floor, knees bent and raised with feet flat on the floor. You can begin with a breast massage to get the yoni lubricated. Once ready, insert your egg and sip it up.

2. On the inhale, you are going to arch your mid-back, rocking your pelvis back toward the floor.

3. On the exhale, you are going to flatten your back against the floor. Gently rock your tailbone toward the ceiling (without lifting hips off the floor), and squeeze the egg with your yoni muscles.

4. As you exhale and squeeze, take one hand and lightly pull the string to add resistance.

5. Continue to play with string as you inhale and exhale with the pelvis rocking motion. Be sure not to pull so hard you take the egg out.

6. See how slow and sensual you can make the movement. Try to hold the squeeze of the egg for 5-10 seconds. Use the sound "HAAAA" as you exhale out.

7. Be sure to circulate the energy in the Microcosmic Orbit, breathing up the back and exhaling down the front in the fire cycle and/or breathing up the front and exhaling down the back in the water cycle. This breath will help move the sexual energy. Try moving sensually, with the pelvis rocking as you breathe energy through the orbit.

★Bonus

*   You can also try keeping the pelvic tilted up, back flat, while you inhale and exhale, sipping the egg up deeper intothe yoni. Try to do nine breaths and relax.

*   Next, try to lift the hips up off the floor and pelvic rock as you squeeze and release the egg. You can lightly tug the string in this position too.

When you have finished the exercise, remove the egg or, if you'd like, wear it throughout the day.

Journal Reflection

Are you beginning to feel sexual energy moving throughout your body? Describe the impact of the exercises on your day-to-day life. What changes, if any, do you feel?

_____

_____

_____

_____

_____

_____

_____

_____

_____

_____

Day 18

Intention: Circulate raw sexual energy through Ovarian Breathing.

As women, we have amazing, beautiful, and complex bodies. While we may give little deliberate thought to our yoni and breasts, we give even less consideration to our ovaries. In today's practice, we bring your awareness to your ovaries by connecting to the raw sexual energy that lies there, bringing it into your womb, and circulating it through the Microcosmic Orbit.

A woman's womb represents her cosmic creative force that extends back to all her female ancestors. The eggs that we release throughout our life during our menstrual cycle, and the ones that get fertilized to become our children, were actually formed when we were a baby inside our mother's womb. In fact, the egg that we came out of was formed inside our grandmother's womb when she was pregnant with our mother. Unlike men who constantly generate sperm, we are born with our lifetime supply of eggs. We come from an egg that was once in our grandmother, and she's from an egg formed inside her grandmother, and so on, and so on. We as women have an infinite connection to the female ancestors in our family and the divine feminine power of birth and creation.

During the reproductive years, women release between 300–500 eggs with an estimated five hundred thousand on reserve in the ovaries. The Taoists recognized the tremendous sexual power that was contained within the ovaries and practiced Ovarian Breathing to tap into that energy. Even if you do not intend to have children, it is still important for you to connect to the power in your ovaries. We have more eggs than we could ever use in this lifetime, and we need not let the energy go to waste. As mentioned in the introduction, the ovaries are the producers of the largest amount of *jing*, and being able to circulate this energy will bring healing physically and spiritually.

Doing the practice of Ovarian Breathing can have many benefits, including lessening the bleeding during menses, reducing cramping, breast soreness, and other PMS symptoms. It has been discovered that the most powerful time to do Ovarian Breathing is the time between the end of a woman's moon cycle and ovulation. As the egg is preparing to descend through the fallopian tubes into the uterus in hopes of getting gestated, it is filled with maximum *jing qi*. This powerful life-giving energy is potent and hot, filled with *yang*, and can be transformed into the higher spiritual centers.

Ovarian Breathing is also important to do if you are celibate or not sexually active. Sexual energy builds up in our reproductive organs and needs to be released. When we repress our sexual energy, we can adversely increase our negative emotions (think of the bitchy woman who you know needs to get laid). Ultimately it can lead to the deterioration of our reproductive and vital organs. Practices like Ovarian Breathing are important because it helps to move the energy, so it doesn't stagnate.

Read these steps several times before trying it. Once you get it, you'll be able to move through the steps quickly.

Steps to Ovarian Breathing

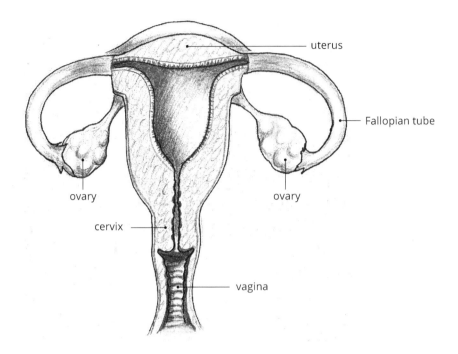

1. Sit up straight with your feet flat on the ground, allowing the Bubbling Spring points on your feet to connect with the earth.

2. Rub your hands together to warm them and awaken the energy points in the center of your palms. Then rub your lower back, massaging your kidneys. Bring warmth into your kidneys as the ruler of *jing*.

3. Next, you must find your ovaries. Like we did during the yoni massage, place your hands in an upside triangle over your womb. Thumbs are touching under your navel, and index fingers touch the tip of your pubic bone. Allow your hands to relax in this position.

4. Where your pinky fingers land is around where your ovaries are. You can feel around for them by pressing gently into your flesh on each side. They should feel like eyeballs underneath the skin.

5. Don't worry if you can't locate them, just close your eyes and imagine them there, like two pink pearls. Inhale into your kidneys and exhale, sending the energy from your kidneys into your ovaries.

6. Next, take a few moments to warm your ovaries by rubbing them in a circular motion with your hands.

7. As you rub your ovaries, slightly open and close your yoni. Imagine it is a flower and very gently pulse it. This should bring warm and tingling sensations to you.

8. Then place your hands back in the triangle. Where the index or pointer fingers land is where the Ovarian Palace or center of your womb is. This is where we will bring the ovarian energy into.

9. Imagine the sexual energy of the ovaries collecting there with a vibrant pink light. Inhale and exhale it into the Ovarian Palace.

10. See the Ovarian Palace filling with pink energy. Pink is the color of sexual energy as it combines the white color of a man's semen (which contains his life force) with the red blood of a woman's menses (which contains her life force).

11. Take a sip of air and move the pink ball of energy to the clitoris. Take another sip of air, move it to the perineum, and take a final tiny sip to move it to the tailbone.

12. Pause for a second and then exhale the energy up the spine to the crown.

13. Circulate the pink energy around the crown nine times counterclockwise, and then reverse it and circulate it nine times clockwise. This revitalizes the mind with creative sexual energy, improves memory, and balances the right and left sides of the brain.

14. Inhale and exhale the energy down the front channel.

15. Practice circulating the Ovarian energy two to three more times.

16. When you are finished, circulate the energy nine times counterclockwise around your navel, then reverse the direction nine times and store it as a pink pearl behind your belly button.

Journal Reflection

1. Were you able to connect with the energy of your ovaries? How did it feel?

   _____

   _____

   _____

   _____

   _____

2. What difference did you feel between circulating *qi* in the Microcosmic Orbit and circulating *jing qi* with Ovarian Breathing?

   _____

   _____

   _____

   _____

   _____

Day 19

Intention: Stimulate sexual energy in the pelvis with dance movements and the yoni egg.

Beautiful goddess, we have been doing some wonderful and deep work moving and circulating our energy. Today we will have some fun combining the new techniques we've learned with the yoni egg and dance. Now that we have some new practices under our belt let's use them in a warm-up. Before you warm up, however, be sure to put your yoni egg in so it's ready for our exercises. Feel free to do a breast massage before inserting the egg to stimulate your sexual energy. You will begin by heating up your inner cauldron or lower tan tien.

As you know, we've been storing our energy behind our navel. This is because there is a power center there that can hold it safely. The lower tan tien is located three finger widths below our navel, right above our pelvis. You can imagine it as a pot or cauldron that you can use to "cook" your spiritual, vital, and sexual essence. It is also the location of the sacral chakra in the Tantra system. The sacral chakra governs our ability to be sensual and enjoy life. When we rub our bellies this way, we awaken life force and sexual energy. This massage is also good for our digestion and elimination system.

Warm-up:

Heating up the Cauldron

Sit up straight or stand with your feet on the floor and take a few deep breaths in and out. Rub 9, 27, or 36 circles in a counterclockwise direction around the navel, getting larger and larger, and then the same number of circles going clockwise, getting smaller and smaller.

Microcosmic Orbit

Place your hands on your lower tan tien sending energy there. Take a deep breath and begin to circulate the energy through the Microcosmic Orbit. Choose to bring it up the front/water channel or back/fire channel. Perhaps try it both ways. Store the energy behind your navel.

Yoni Eggercise 1: Make it Clap

With our energy fully circulated, we are now going to begin our yoni egg practice. We will practice isolating the sides of the yoni and bringing the walls of the yoni together. I call this "making it clap."

1. Do a few yoni breaths. Breathe into her and contract your yoni muscle, exhale and relax.

2. Then, in your mind's eye, imagine the right side of your yoni. Breathe in, squeeze it. Exhale and relax.

3. See the left side of your yoni. Inhale and squeeze it, exhale and let it go.

4. Now, place your hands in front of you about six inches apart as if you are about to clap.

5. Your hands represent the right and left sides of your yoni.

6. Take a deep breath in. On the exhale, try to bring the walls of your yoni to touch while simultaneously bringing the palms of the hands together like you are clapping. Inhale and separate.

7. Do this at least nine times. You can also do three sets of nine if you feel comfortable with it.

Yoni Eggercise 2: Rock Steady and Wine

After we made it clap with our egg, let's circulate our sexual energy by dancing with our egg. I suggest playing some sensual music. My favorite music to do this to is reggae. It can be fast, slow, or mid-tempo, as long as it makes you feel sexy.

1. Be sure you are standing. You should have a slight bend in your knees. On the inhale, you are going to arch your back and rock your pelvis back. Try to isolate your pelvic bowl, so it is just that moving and not your ribs.

2. On the exhale, you are going to thrust your pelvis forward.

3. As you are doing this back and forth movement, squeeze your egg as you exhale your pelvis forward. Let it go when you inhale back. Do this at least nine times.

4. Now we are going to "wine" our waist. Imagine there is a string hanging from your tailbone. Move the string in a circle with your tailbone. This will help you isolate your pelvis and hips as you move them around in a circle. Squeeze the egg while you do this. Make sure you circle both to the left and the right.

5. This dance is called 'the wine' in the Caribbean. It awakens your root and sacral chakras. Practice wining slow and wining fast. Bend your knees and wine down to the ground, and then wine up. Have fun!

6. When you are finished, circulate the energy in the Microcosmic Orbit and store it behind your navel.

Wear your egg throughout the day if you can. Practice the various ways to work with the egg when you have free time. You can give little squeezes while at work, shopping, etc., and no one has to know!

Journal Reflection

1. Are you noticing any differences in your egg practice? Are your muscles getting stronger? Is your yoni feeling more sensitive? Describe any progress or results you are getting from working with the egg.

_____

_____

_____

_____

_____

2. Do you feel your sexual energy getting stronger? Are you more energized? Note changes you have in your libido, creativity, or energy level.

_____

_____

_____

_____

_____

Day 20

Intention: Raise sexual energy through vaginal weight lifting.

Today we step up our sexual energy cultivation with some advanced yoni egg kung fu!

Yes, dear goddess, if you have been doing the work for these last three weeks, now is the time to go to the next level. Prepare to "enter the dragon" with vaginal weight lifting!

In this exercise, we will use our yoni egg with a weight hanging from it for added resistance. Creating a weight is pretty simple as you can use:

• Another drilled egg if you have one or
• Fill the bag your yoni egg came in or another small bag with a few teaspoons of dried beans or rice.

(I do NOT recommend trying to actually hang 5-pound weights etc., from your yoni as I've seen some internet sensations do. You can really damage your body this way. We don't need incredible hulk yonis; we must balance strength with being supple and soft.)

This exercise is done standing and will energize and strengthen your whole system, including your core muscles. It will send the sexual energy up to your higher spiritual centers and core channel. Make sure you have your weight attached to a long string that reaches below your knees, so you have space enough to swing. This is best done nude or with a long skirt and no underwear.

Warm-up

Begin with a nice, sensual breast massage to help stimulate your sexual energy. Practice your Ovarian Breathing a few times to get the *jing* moving.

Vaginal Weight Lifting Steps

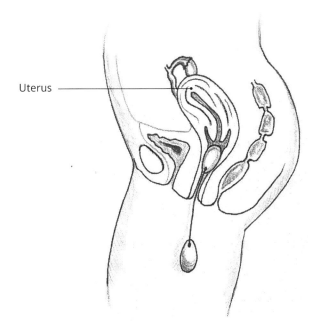

Uterus

1. Loop a string through your yoni egg. Make sure that it is at least 18-20 inches long.

2. Tie the string hanging from your yoni egg to the weight.

3. Stand up, holding onto the weight.

4. Slowly and gently let the weight go, allowing it to hang between your legs.

5. Imagine you are sucking up the weight with your core muscles between your navel and spine. Activate the lower tan tien.

6. Try to breathe normally while at the same time holding the weight between your legs with your vaginal and core muscles.

7. Using only your yoni muscles, begin to swing the egg in a circle. Do this without moving any other body part. Make sure your feet are firmly planted, and knees comfortably bent. This may take some practice to do successfully, so be patient.

8. Experiment with rocking the sacrum back and forth. This movement will cause the weight to swing back and forth. Keep the movement internal and small.

9. If you're able to hold the egg and weight while rocking your sacrum, try other movements like figure eights, circling the hips, wining, dancing, etc.

10. When you complete your practice, remove the egg and weight, and don't forget to store your sexual energy in a pink pearl behind your navel.

Journal Reflection

1. Describe your experience of vaginal weight lifting. Were you able to hold the weight? For how long?

    _____

    _____

    _____

    _____

    _____

2. Reflect on your journey of sexual kung fu so far (kung fu means skills achieved through practice and hard work). What have these exercises taught you about yourself?

    _____

    _____

    _____

    _____

    _____

Day 21

Intention: Take a Sexy Goddess Bath.

Congratulations, beautiful! You have completed week 3 of *WET: 30-Day Deep Dive Into Sensual Bliss and Feminine Pleasure.* You have worked hard, and now it's time to relax! We will complete this week with another signature bath.

Ingredients:

1. Yellow and pink flowers petals (colors reflect sexual attraction and fertility)

2. 5 drops of your favorite sweet-smelling essential oils like rose, geranium, orange, sandalwood, and/or jasmine, etc.

3. 1 cup of honey

4. Yellow and pink candles

5. Sweet-smelling incense

Sexy Goddess Bath instructions

- Burn yellow and pink candles and sweet incense. Make it a sensual experience.

- Run your bath water as hot as you like it. When it is about half full, add the honey, tasting it first to make your essence sweet, and then add the oils.

- Once it is full, sprinkle two handfuls of flower petals into the bath.

- State your intentions into the water and get in.

- As you are in the bath, massage your body, including your breasts and yoni, with the water and flower petals. Massage your ovaries and Ovarian Palace.

- Pay special attention to your womb. Massage in large circles going clockwise, starting under your ribs and moving to your pelvis, bringing the circles in smaller and smaller until you get to your navel.

- Add a bit of firm pressure over your abdomen to stimulate peristalsis so you can later release any contents in your intestines adding pressure on top of your womb.

- Place your hands on your womb and ask her to release anything she needs to let go of. Use the healing sounds or any intuitive sounds you'd like to make to release. This can be a powerful experience as we hold emotions in our womb. If you feel the need to cry, let it happen. It may also arouse sexual feelings. Pleasure yourself if you desire to.

- When you finish, lightly pat yourself dry, allowing some of the flower petals to stick to your skin until they naturally fall off.

Have a beautiful evening!

Journal Reflection

Write an ode to your inner sexy goddess. Write words praising her for her strength and beauty. Use the prompt, "I am a sexy badass goddess…"

_____

_____

_____

_____

_____

_____

_____

_____

_____

_____

WEEK 4:

ORGASMIC

Introduction

"Orgasm is a state where your body is no more felt as matter; it vibrates like energy, electricity. It vibrates so deeply, from the very foundation, that you completely forget that it is a material thing. It becomes an electric phenomenon..."

—Osho

What exactly is an orgasm? The above quote is from Osho, a Tantric mystic from the 21st century. However, being transformed into an energetic "electric phenomenon" during orgasm is not what most of us experience. Here's Webster's dictionary definition of orgasm and the more common understanding:

orgasm -

1. (n) an explosive discharge of neuromuscular tensions at the height of sexual arousal that is usually accompanied by the ejaculation of semen in the male and by vaginal contractions in the female

2. (v) to climax from sexual excitement, characterized by feelings of pleasure centered in the genitals and (in men) experienced as an accompaniment to ejaculation

It is obvious that Webster did not practice Tantra. In the realms of sacred sexuality, orgasm is much more. The following excerpt is from a short story I wrote based on my first Tantric sexual experience with a lover. It is called "My First Time". You can read it in its entirety in the final section of this book.

"I don't know what you're-" His lips swallowed whatever words I was trying to get out. The levy of passion broke open between us, and we became swept away in the flood. He went from being on his back to being between my legs. All six foot eight of him laced his body on top of me... I wrapped my legs around his waist. He kissed me like he wanted to devour me, and I let out ecstatic moans, happily being consumed. Moving from my mouth, he began savoring my neck, eventually moving down to explore the rest of me. Cupping my breasts in his hands, he gently licked my nipples; I lit up like a tree on Christmas Eve. I felt orgasmic energy in every pore of my body. It was as if my skin wanted to drink him. I never wanted anyone as much as I wanted him in that moment...

It felt as if my entire body was a yoni; he began to kiss and lick up and down my spine. Is this what kundalini feels like? I could feel the energy surging up my back as if my spine was one long clitoris. I couldn't believe I was feeling this way and this man hadn't even penetrated me! The funny thing was, I did have a sexual partner at this time, a man named Kenneth. In fact, I had great love for Kenneth, yet I had never felt this way with him. With Jelani, I felt desire for him in every cell of my body and orgasmic waves that pulsated through my entire being. In the case of Kenneth, my sexual pleasure seemed to be located primarily in my genitals, and while it was good, it wasn't this good. I felt like he wanted me to perform for him. I did most of the work while he laid back and "took it". With Jelani, I completely surrendered into the fire of his passion. This wasn't him "fucking" me either like the porn stars try to do. This was completely something else. This was the god worshiping the goddess…

Prior to this experience, I did not know that my entire body could be orgasmic in lovemaking. My lover, whom I call "Jelani," gave me a sexual experience I did not know existed. Not only was I capable of having orgasms dance all over my body, but lovemaking could be a spiritual experience. The day following our sacred coitus, I moved about the world in a pink, sparkly bubble - almost devoid of thought. It was as if my whole being had been washed, elevated and reborn. Having "regular" sex with someone became completely unsatisfying and downright frustrating after my Tantric baptism.

The type of whole-body orgasmic experience I had with Jelani, however, is uncommon, and unfortunately, for many women, so is having an orgasm at all. Statistics state that 75 percent of women do not reach orgasm from vaginal penetration alone: sex toys, hands, or tongue are needed. About 10-15 percent of women never reach climax, regardless of the scenario. A 2016 study done by the Archives of Sexual Behavior that surveyed 52,500 adults in the U.S. found that 95 percent of heterosexual men reported they usually or always orgasmed during sex while only 65 percent of heterosexual women did (lesbian women were found to orgasm about 75 percent of the time).

The female orgasm has been called "mysterious" and "elusive" by researchers who don't understand the orgasm gap that exists between many men and women. Perhaps viewing this phenomenon from a sacred sexual lens would be helpful. Many modern women live their daily lives stressed out, closed off, and shut down. A woman constantly battered by this state with no reprieve does not have the energy resources to be orgasmic. All her *qi* is being drained out of her. While many men have sex and orgasm to find relaxation, women tend to be the opposite. Because our nature is *yin*, we must be relaxed and feel safe *first* in order to be orgasmic. We have to slow down and move from a place of rest to fully expand into our orgasmic nature.

Researchers have confirmed that stress activates a woman's flight or fight response, and her vagina shuts down. Blood flow is restricted as the body gets ready to "throw down" or run away. If only 25 percent of women are regularly having orgasms from penetrative sex, I would venture to say that even fewer are having healing, transformative and spiritual climaxes. Most of us are only scratching the surface of sex.

While this book focuses mainly on solo practices, it is the ability to be fully orgasmic in one's own body prior to uniting with another that will make the couple experience even more satisfying. This week we will explore the various kinds of orgasms we are capable of having within our body. Yes, we have a menu of different kinds of orgasms we can choose from at any time during our sensual experiences. Experts cite that women are capable of having anywhere from 4-11 different types of orgasms. This week we will explore five: breast, clitoral, g-spot, organs, and full body. Through this exploration of our own erotic selves, we will know how to open our bodies fully with a beloved. The journey into our orgasmic potential is truly a liberating one; as we learn what turns us on, we begin to not settle for anything less: not only in the bedroom but in our life.

As you approach the practices this week, know that they are for your healing, bliss, and enlightenment. Try not to have a goal-centered approach to the exercises. Don't make "orgasm" a reward or something you have to work for; this is true in sex too. We are naturally orgasmic when we relax and melt open. If you can do this with yourself, you can do it with a partner. Don't force. Open, receive, swell, melt, and be dissolved.

Items Needed for Orgasmic Week

- ½ gallon of milk (You can use coconut, goat's, or whole cow's milk. Whatever your preference.)

- 1 cup of honey

- 10 drops sandalwood essential oil or another sweet oil or perfume

- Two handfuls or more of flower petals (You won't need flowers until the end of the week, see the last exercise. Color is your choice.)

- Natural massage oil

- Yoni Egg

- Organic cucumber or crystal yoni wand

Week 4: Orgasmic

Quote for the week:

"In deep orgasm, if you are aware, you will know for the first time what ecstasy is. Otherwise, you have only heard the word… if your flame of awareness is burning bright, you will be able to know that sex is not just sex. Sex is the outermost layer; deep inside is love; and even deeper is prayer; and deepest is God himself. Sex can become a cosmic experience; then it is tantra…"

—Osho

Day 22

Intention: Reflect on your most orgasmic experience.

Have you ever been fucked open to God? Sorry, maybe I should be more flowery and romantic. Have you ever been made love to so good that you were high-fiving angels? As we begin the last week of our sacred sexual deep dive, I ask that you reflect on the most orgasmic experience you've ever had. This could be with someone else, or it could have been with yourself. Remember, being orgasmic is **not** about the destination; it is about the journey. So even if you are one of the many women who do not regularly experience orgasms during intercourse, reflect on a time when you felt fully connected and alive during lovemaking or another juicy experience.

Orgasmic Reflection

- Close your eyes and try to remember your best orgasmic experience. See it in your imagination first. (This is not about the other person either, but what was awakened in your body.)

- Connect to it with your five senses. What did it taste like, feel like, smell like, sound like and look like?

- What made it particularly orgasmic?

- When you finish recalling, write a short reflection describing it in full color and why it was so amazing for you.

Journal Reflection

1. What do you require to feel safe enough to let go sexually and be orgasmic?

   _____

   _____

   _____

   _____

   _____

2. Are you in tune with what your body desires? Are you comfortable with voicing your needs with your partner/s? Why or why not?

   _____

   _____

   _____

   _____

   _____

Day 23

Intention: Explore the orgasmic potential of the clitoris.

We will begin the orgasmic journey of our body by meeting and getting to know Ms. Clit, aka your clitoris! We call her "Ms." as a title of respect because she is too often ignored or underestimated when it comes to sexual arousal in women.

Ms. Clit is tucked between the inner folds of the labia at the top of the vulva below the pubic bone. The distance between the opening of the yoni and Ms. Clit will vary amongst women. For some women, it is only one or two finger widths, and for other women, it is four finger widths. The little button of pleasure, or "bliss pearl," as the Taoists call it, that sticks out through the inner labia is only the tip of the iceberg. The interior system of erectile tissue spreads across the pelvis and has legs that run down to the vaginal opening. In fact, women have the same amount of erectile tissue as men, with ours being mostly internal. During arousal, the vestibular bulbs become engorged with blood, and we become internally erect. When we orgasm, this blood is released into the circulatory system of our body.

Ms. Clit packs a powerful punch with 8,000 nerve endings, while the penis only has 4,000. The powerful sensations from the clitoris can actually affect about 15,000 nerve endings during arousal. She is the only organ in the human body designed strictly for pleasure; there is no reason for her to be there other than to make us feel good. She also grows! At the onset of puberty, she increases in size, and by time puberty is over, she will be almost twice as big. By the time a woman is 32, the clitoris will be four times larger than it was when she started puberty. Post-menopause, she will be seven times longer than she was at birth. Yes, ladies, getting older makes you even more orgasmic!

It is estimated that about 70 percent of women need direct clitoral stimulation to reach their peak during sex. A clitoral orgasm is the most common orgasm experienced by the majority of women. This orgasm allows a woman to connect to her body's natural ability to physically experience pleasure. It is usually quick, exciting, and awakens a rush of sex hormones. The clitoris also has reflexology zones for the glands of the endocrine system. By connecting to the clitoral orgasm, we open up the body to experience deeper orgasmic bliss.

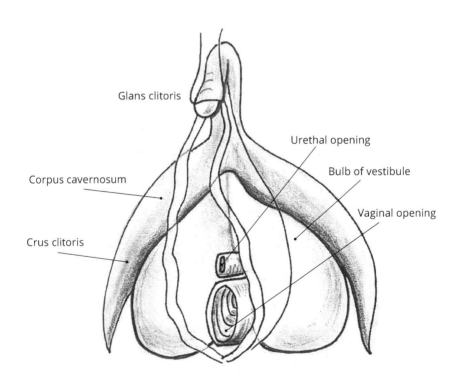

Glans clitoris

Urethral opening

Bulb of vestibule

Corpus cavernosum

Vaginal opening

Crus clitoris

Ms. Clit Exploration

- To begin, start with a breast massage to stir up the sexual energy.

- Next, give yourself a yoni massage. Be sure to use a natural oil and lovingly massage around the pubis mound, inner thighs, and labia until you get to the clitoris. Be sure to move slowly and touch gently.

- Explore your clitoris, but not with the goal of orgasm. The point here is not to "rub one out." Avoid overstimulating her with vigorous friction-based movements or electrical vibrators. While many women do get pleasure from sex toys, overuse can actually deaden the nerve endings there, making one have to work harder and harder to feel stimulation over time.

- You can take out a mirror and look at her. Focus on her and notice what sensations you feel. Move her gently right, left, up and down, and around like the hands of a clock. See if you can feel the surrounding nerve endings that spread through the pelvis and vaginal opening.

- You can also use your yoni egg to stimulate Ms. Clit. Give her a massage with the tip of your egg.

- Breathe in and out deeply, using sounds and sending the orgasmic energy through the Microcosmic Orbit.

- If, while you are exploring, an orgasm happens, allow it. Notice the way a clitoral orgasm feels.

- Store the energy behind your navel when you are finished.

Journal Reflection

1. Describe the experience of exploring Ms. Clit. How does she like to be touched? Are you aware of her when you have sex? How can you bring her more into your lovemaking?

    _____

    _____

    _____

    _____

    _____

2. Are you familiar with the way a clitoral orgasm feels? Try gently exploring Ms. Clit and let her have an orgasm. Maybe ask your partner to help you. Describe the sensations you feel during and after.

    _____

    _____

    _____

    _____

    _____

Week 4: Orgasmic

Day 24

Intention: Awaken healing orgasmic energy in the breasts.

Today we are going to explore another one of the many different types of orgasms we can have: breast orgasm. Yes, you can have an orgasm in your bells of love! Imagine the breasts as wings of the heart. When we pleasure and send loving healing energy to our breasts, we also send healing energy to our heart chakra. The heart center is the active pole of energy in women, where we give from, while our yoni is the passive or receptive pole, where we receive from. In men, it is the opposite; they receive in their heart center and give through their penis or lingam. When these energy centers are lined up in lovemaking, the energy circulates between the lovers in a perfect circle of masculine and feminine balance. As the active center, the breasts have the ability to awaken the whole body to orgasm.

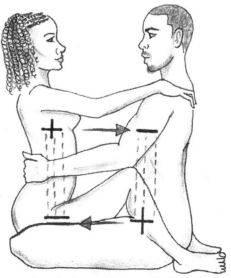

Couple Sacred Energy Exchange

Before you begin, insert your yoni egg to enhance the sensations in your vagina and get a double workout as it massages the reflexology zones. If you have a rose quartz egg, it would be especially good for this as it emits frequencies of self-love to the heart chakra. Sip the egg up deeply toward the reflexology zone of the heart.

Breast Orgasm Exploration

1. Sit up with your back straight and your feet flat on the floor or lie on your back on your bed. Take several deep breaths. Practice the Microcosmic Orbit meditation several times, breathing either up the water channel and down the fire channel or vice versa.

2. Bring your attention to your breasts. Place your hands there and imagine breathing in a soft pink light. Allow the light to expand with the breath into both breasts. Contract your yoni muscles a few times. Feel the orgasmic energy swirl there.

3. Place your left hand over your heart and place your right hand on your yoni. Begin to exchange energy between your heart/ breasts and yoni through the breath. Imagine pink energy flowing from the heart/breast to the yoni.

4. Stroke up the midline with your hands from the yoni and bring both hands to the breasts. Give yourself a breast massage. Practice breathing into the breasts, relaxing, and melting into them. Allow yourself to touch gently and softly, enjoying the sensual feeling of caressing your breast.

5. As you massage your breasts, notice how the yoni becomes aroused. Give your yoni egg a few squeezes as you massage your breasts. Feel the orgasmic energy awaken in your breasts. Breathe into the breast and feel the orgasmic energy expand. Breath is the key to orgasm. You may notice a circulation of sexual energy between your breast and yoni.

6. Allow yourself to explore your nipples and see if you feel them connect to Ms. Clit. There is a connection between our nipples and our clitoris. You may be able to orgasm from nipple stimulation alone. Try massaging your nipples with the centers of your palms in a circle. Try wetting them with your saliva and gently twirling them between your fingertips. The nipples, like the clitoris, will awaken the endocrine glands and help balance your hormones. In lovemaking, be gentle with the nipples, so they stay sensitive to orgasmic pleasure.

7. Continue to explore the juicy sensation of breathing, massaging, and awakening the sexual energy in the breasts and nipples. Breathe the breasts open and expand in self-love. Feel free to bring yourself to climax or do whatever feels good. Try to orgasm without touching the yoni and only caressing your breast. However, if you like, you can pleasure both the clitoris and breast into climax.

8. Store the sexual energy behind your navel by circulating it until it is a small pink pearl.

Journal Reflection

1. The breasts are the key to awakening orgasm in women. Do you stimulate your breasts or allow them to be stimulated when having sex? Are you able to feel a connection between your breasts and yoni?

_____

_____

_____

_____

_____

2. Our breasts connect to our heart center. When it comes to the heart, are you primarily a giver or receiver? Reflect on the ways you can learn to both give and receive love through the heart center.

_____

_____

_____

_____

_____

Day 25

Intention: Explore our sacred Goddess Spot.

Next stop on the orgasmic train is our sacred goddess spot, known as the g-spot. Thought to be a myth for some time, the g-spot actually exists. You can find it by lying down on your back with your legs open. Insert your middle finger into your yoni and stroke on the upper front wall like you are gesturing "come hither." The texture of it will feel different than the rest of the wall. It should feel like a little ridged bump.

Very often, the g-spot can feel numb or painful when touched either with a finger or during sex. This is usually because it is holding onto emotion or stagnant *qi*. The key to awakening the g-spot is to be relaxed and very aroused. During intercourse, when the g-spot gets stimulated, we will very often feel like we have to pee. It swells up like a sponge with fluid from the skene's glands, the female prostate. It is believed that this is where female ejaculation fluid comes from. In Tantra, female ejaculation is considered to be amrita or divine nectar. Female ejaculation or "squirting" has become sensationalized in porn, but it is really the embodiment of a woman's *yin* essence as she opens the gates of her jade fountain, allowing her sacred waters to flow.

In exploring our goddess spot, we do it not with the intention to "squirt" but to allow ourselves to release any tension or emotion that may be there. If, in that process, the waters wish to flow, let them. In releasing the blockages, we open ourselves to experience the healing of the g-spot orgasm. The goddess spot orgasm is cleansing, helps heal negative emotions, awakens passion, and bonds us to our lover (or self).

Goddess Spot Exploration

Depending on how long your vaginal canal is, you may or may not be able to reach your g-spot with your fingers alone. If you measure the distance between your clitoris and vaginal opening, this will give you an idea of where your g-spot is located: opposite the clitoris on the inside wall.

You can use a natural lubricant like organic raw coconut oil and explore your g-spot with your fingers, or you can try one of the following:

- Peeled organic cucumber (Cucumbers actually help cleanse the vaginal canal. See Bonus Exercise 2 for more information.)

- Crystal wand (These are 4–5-inch wands made out of crystals like rose quartz. They run between $40-$100+, depending on the type.)

I am aware some women like working with sex toys such as dildos, vibrators etc. If you do, please use ones made from organic or natural materials. Personally, I do not put anything unnatural or plastic into my yoni as it can leave chemicals inside the vagina. Use your discretion when inserting anything into your sacred yoni. You can also have a partner help you with the following exercise.

Steps to G-spot Exploration

1. Before you begin, make sure your bladder is empty.

2. After you select which tool you'd like to massage the g-spot with, lie on your back with your legs open in a relaxed position.

Breathe deeply in and out, circulating the energy in the Microcosmic Orbit a few times.

3. Give yourself a breast massage and yoni massage until you are very aroused. Feel free to imagine your sexual fantasy.

4. Then lubricate the tool you plan to use to massage your g-spot. Take a deep breath, and slowly, with intention, insert it into your yoni.

5. If using your fingers, feel around the upper wall for a spongy bump. Make the "come here" motion by curling your middle finger. When you press into it, it may feel painful, numb, like you have to pee or be pleasurable.

6. If working with another object, such as the cucumber or wand, try to sense when it is rubbing your g-spot. Notice the sensation, whether numb, painful, or pleasurable.

7. Continue to massage the g-spot, noticing whatever sensation you have without judgment. Ask your inner goddess if there is anything she needs to release there in order to open to her full orgasmic potential.

8. As you listen and massage, try releasing any emotion there with the healing sounds:
   - SSSSSSS: sadness/grief
   - TCHOOO: fear
   - SHHHHH: anger
   - HAAAAAWW: anxiety, impatience
   - WOOOOO: worry
   - HEEEEEEE: energetic imbalances

9. If any tears come while doing the sounds, release and allow them. Memories may come back to you as you tap into the subconscious. Breathe and let go through the sounds.

10. If massaging the g-spot brings pleasure, release moans. Try these sounds: mmmmmm, ooooooooohhhhh, ahhhhhhhh.

11. If you feel the desire to climax during this, then allow yourself; it may be a great emotional release as the g-spot orgasm is much deeper than the clitoral.

12. Circulate the energy and store it behind your navel.

Journal Reflection

1. Describe the sensations you experienced while exploring your goddess spot. Was it pleasurable, numb, or painful? Did the sensation change by the end of the exercise?

_____

_____

_____

_____

_____

2. Did any emotions or memories come up for you? If so, what were they? Were you able to release them through the sound?

_____

_____

_____

_____

_____

Day 26

Intention: Send orgasmic energy to your organs.

I hear your thoughts. *Say what? What the heck is an organ orgasm?*

Throughout our practice, we have discussed how the Taoists associate certain emotions with the major organs of our bodies. We have released the negative emotion with the healing sounds through various exercises. Now, however, we will cultivate the positive emotion of each organ by wrapping it in orgasmic energy.

Through organ orgasm, we will fortify and restore the virtues of each organ. As you circulate sexual energy around each organ, it will greatly benefit your health and inspire more joy and happiness. It will feel like each organ is a little pocket of beaming light. The vital organs of the lungs, kidney, liver, heart, and spleen are filled with life force energy. This is why the Ancient Egyptians saved some of these organs in canopic jars when they interred their deceased. They knew they were important and wanted to preserve them for the afterlife.

Follow the instructions below to experience organ orgasm. You can also apply this in lovemaking and send healing orgasmic energy to your vital organs while having sex.

Organ Orgasm Exploration

1. Before we begin, you must get your sexual energy flowing. Give yourself a breast or yoni massage to reach arousal. Bring yourself to between 50 and 60 percent arousal (100 percent being the point of climax).

2. Once you are at the halfway point, contract the left and right sides of the anus and bring the sexual energy to the left and right ovaries. Breathe it down and around the Microcosmic Orbit.

3. Breathe the sexual energy to the ovaries again and move it between the left and right kidneys. Wrap the sexual energy around the kidneys nine times, cultivating the energy of peace. Close the opening of the yoni to pull the sexual energy up into the kidneys. See them glow blue. Use your imagination and the breath to guide the energy there. Exhale and relax.

4. Breathe in again, close the opening of the yoni and send the sexual energy to the lungs. Visualize them sparkling white. Wrap them with energy nine times, nourishing your ability to let go and increased confidence. Exhale and release.

5. On the next breath, squeeze the yoni closed and send the sexual energy to the liver. Fill it with the color green and wrap it nine times, waking up the quality of kindness and self-expansion. Breathe out and relax.

6. Breathe in, contract the yoni and send the energy to the heart. See it glow a vibrant red. Send the energy around nine times, cultivating joy and love. Exhale and let it go.

7. Next, take a deep breath, close the yoni, and send the energy to the spleen. Visualize it yellow. Wrap it nine times, nurturing trust and compassion. Exhale and relax.

8. Once you have finished sending orgasmic energy to each organ, circulate the energy in the Microcosmic Orbit, storing it behind the navel.

Journal Reflection

1. Reflect on your experience circulating orgasmic energy around your organs. Was it mostly your imagination, or were you able to feel sexual energy in and around your organs? Describe the sensations you felt.

   _____

   _____

   _____

   _____

   _____

2. Go back and look at the positive virtues of each organ. Which quality do you think you most need to work on?

   _____

   _____

   _____

   _____

   _____

Day 27

Intention: Open the body to multiple and full-body orgasms.

There is a French saying that calls the orgasm "la petite mort" or "little death." This is aligned with Tantric thought. In the midst of orgasm, the false self "dies" and falls away, and we get to revel in the True Self. We experience the transcendence of the physical body and the merging of the Self back into the unity of Universal Consciousness. When we are in the midst of orgasm, there is no thought: one of the major goals of meditation. Our minds are clear, our bodies caught in rapture, and we merge with ultimate bliss. This is why we may experience tears during sex as our lovers open us up to the Divine. A beautiful death it is, and we taste for a brief moment what heaven is.

Today we will take our orgasm to the next level by exploring full-body orgasm. The techniques you will practice today have the potential to open you up to multiple orgasms by yourself or with a partner. As women, we have the advantage in Tantric sex. Our goal is to relax and expand our orgasmic level so we can reach higher and higher levels of spiritual bliss. We have a greater orgasmic capacity than men, with the ability to ride our orgasms like waves, climbing higher and higher and languishing in quiet lulls. Men, on the other hand, must learn to separate orgasm from ejaculation and maintain an erection for a longer period of time so that the sexual experience does not end prematurely. Men can become multi-orgasmic, too; it just requires more discipline as they lose life force energy with ejaculation. Having an orgasm does not drain our life force. Men must learn to control and direct; we must learn to relax and open. When both parties can do this, the sexual energy can be cycled up to the higher spiritual centers giving the gift of a physical and spiritual orgasm.

Choose a time of day to do this when you have enough time and will be undisturbed. This isn't about getting a "quickie" in; you need space to play and explore. We will work with bandhas or power locks. When you apply a bandha, you hold or tighten a part of the body. This helps to collect and direct the energy. You may need to read over this several times and practice the locks prior to moving the sexual energy, so it begins to become automatic.

Full Body Orgasm Exploration

1. Begin with a sensual massage of the breasts, clitoris, and yoni. Use all that you've learned so far to get yourself very aroused. It may be best to try this sitting up in a chair at first with your feet flat on the floor. This allows you to direct the energy upward. If you cannot relax this way, you can lie down on your back, with your knees raised and bent and feet flat on the floor.

2. When you are at about 50-60 percent arousal, gently squeeze the entrance of the yoni closed. This will prevent the sexual energy from leaking.

3. Next, you're going to apply your first set of locks, which activate the sacral pump. Pumps are located at several places along the spine and help to direct the sexual energy up.

4. Keeping the yoni closed, take a sip of air and curl toes under, tighten the muscles of your butt and thighs and tuck in your tailbone. You can contract your anus to send a jet of sexual energy up the spine. Hold.

5. Next, activate the cranial pump by closing your fists, tucking the chin in, and pressing the tongue against the roof of your mouth. Sip the sexual energy up the spine to the crown.

6. Continue holding the breath and circulate the energy around the crown nine times.

7. You can also direct the energy up to the crown with your eyes. Allow both eyes to flutter up as if you are looking at the third eye in the center of your forehead.

8. Exhale down the front of the body, release all the bandhas, and relax.

9. With the release of the locks, you may feel orgasmic energy move up the pumps along your spine or move in waves all over your body. Allow yourself to breathe in and out for a few moments. Rest and feel the energy.

10. Practice this twice more, bringing yourself to 75 percent arousal and then practice again at 85 percent arousal. Be sure to relax between each round and allow yourself to feel the energy moving.

11. Imagine the orgasmic energy expanding through every cell in your body when you release it. Send love and healing to every part of you with your juicy, orgasmic energy.

12. Use your mind to direct the sexual energy to different parts of the body: your arms, legs, breasts, lips, liver, spleen, etc. Notice where the energy moves on its own. Allow yourself to release through sounds.

13. Feel free to bring yourself to full climax using this technique. Be sure to circulate your energy in the Microcosmic Orbit several times, so the energy does not get stuck in your head. You can also brush it down from your heart to your lower tan tien.

14. When you finish, circulate it nine times counterclockwise, getting bigger and bigger and then clockwise, getting smaller and smaller. Store the energy as a pink pearl behind your navel.

Journal Reflection

1. What does a full-body orgasm mean to you? Describe your experience exploring full-body orgasm and the power locks.

_____

_____

_____

_____

_____

2. For a woman to be orgasmic, she has to let go. Are you becoming more comfortable with surrender, not only in the bedroom but in your life? What are the ways you can let go more?

_____

_____

_____

_____

_____

Day 28

Intention: Have an orgasmic bath.

Goddess, you are amazing!

You have committed to four weeks of nourishing and cultivating your sacred sexual energy. Today you will take your final bath for our deep dive, sealing off the week of connecting to your orgasmic power.

We will be using milk and honey in this bath; both ingredients will soften and nourish your skin, leaving it supple and sweet.

Ingredients:

- ½ gallon of milk (You can use coconut, goat's, or whole cow's milk. Whatever your preference.)
- 1 cup of honey
- 10 drops sandalwood essential oil or another sweet oil or perfume
- 2 handfuls or more of flower petals

The type of flower and color will depend on what energy you'd like to cultivate.

Here is a basic way of categorizing by color:

White - peace, calm, and purity
Pink - love, romance, and hope
Red - passion, courage, and vitality
Blue - healing, tranquility, and wisdom
Green - healing, fertility, and abundance
Yellow - creativity, confidence, and energy
Orange - warmth, balance, and happiness
Purple - luck, power, and success

You may want to try just going to a flower shop and seeing what flowers speak to you. You can even mix several different colors together; follow your inner wisdom.

To make the orgasmic bath:

- Run the water to the temperature you like.

- You can burn candles and incense to enhance the atmosphere (Apply same color association to candles).

- When the tub is about halfway, pour your ingredients into the bathwater.

- Always say your affirmations and prayers as you put in the ingredients.

Here are some affirmations you can use:

1. I am a free, orgasmic, and sacred sexual woman.

2. My yoni is multi-orgasmic, healing, and holy. Whoever has the privilege to enter her is blessed. I attract partners who love me the way I want, need, and deserve to be loved.

3. I am a blessed daughter of The Goddess; there is nothing to fear.

4. I forgive myself for all past mistakes and love myself unconditionally.

5. I am an orgasmic being, living an orgasmic life.
   - Soak in the bath for at least 30 minutes.

- Pray and meditate. Recite the above affirmations while in the tub.

- Massage your body with the milk- and honey-infused water. Enjoy how soft and slippery your skin feels.

- Play with some of the different types of orgasms while in the bath. You can massage your breast with milk and honey, sending orgasmic waves throughout your entire body.

- You can also use your yoni egg while in the bathtub for some added bathtub bliss. You can play with the string attached to your egg and strum it like a guitar, allow the vibrations to send pleasure through your yoni.

- Spend the evening doing something that makes you feel like a goddess!

- Maybe a nice long yoni egg practice, making love, watching a favorite romantic movie, or just going to sleep.

Journal Entry

Write a poem or sketch a picture that explores orgasmic energy. Use the title "An Ode to Orgasm."

Bonus Exercise

Day 29

Intention: Allow your yoni to get some vitamin D.

Our first bonus exercise invites you to give your yoni some vitamin D. No, not that vitamin D! We will try the Taoist practice of Sunning! In this practice, you open your legs and allow your yoni to bask in the sun. By exposing our darkest and most *yin* part of our body to *yang* sunlight, we help bring healing and energetic balance to our yoni. The natural sunlight tones muscles, fills us with vitamin D, and kills bacteria.

Tips for Sunning

- If you have a private backyard or outside area, lie on your back, either naked or wearing a long skirt and no underwear. Open your legs to expose your yoni to the sunlight. You can sit in reclined goddess pose with your legs open and the soles of the feet touching. This helps the energy circulate.

- If it's wintertime, or you don't have access to a private outdoor area, you can pull back the blinds or shades in your house in a spot that gets a lot of sunlight. Set yourself up in front of the window (mindful of the neighbors, of course) and practice sunning. Feel free to use pillows to get comfortable; you can place them under your legs and back for support.

- While lying there, use your hands to open your labia, to expose the deep folds of the yoni to the sunlight. Imagine she is a flower opening.

- Relax with the breath and imagine your yoni drinking up that good *yang* solar energy. The energy will be absorbed by the ovaries, and it has a very soothing effect on the reproductive system. This part of our body rarely, if ever, gets sunlight.

- Circulate the energy in the Microcosmic Orbit. Enjoy the warmth of the sun in your jade fountain as it breaks up stagnant energy. You may even begin to feel orgasmic from the sun's penetration. Once I had an orgasm just from the sun on my yoni!

- If you can, also enjoy the rays of the sun on your exposed breast. This can be really juicy too.

- I also like to drink the sunlight into my third eye, located in the middle of the forehead between the eyebrows. Awakening the third eye ignites inner wisdom, intuition, and spiritual vision.

Journal Reflection

1. Describe how it felt to get that natural vitamin D in your yoni?

_____

_____

_____

_____

_____

2. Did you notice any difference in your energy or sensations once you were done?

_____

_____

_____

_____

_____

Bonus Exercise 2

Day 30

Intention: Clean the yoni internally with a cucumber cleanse.

I'm going to share with you a fun and healing exercise to cleanse the yoni. This comes from the teachings of the White Tigress women in China who used sexual energy cultivation practices to attain "immortality." All you need is a cucumber; buy an organic one as it will be inserted internally.

Cucumber Cleansing

The type of vaginal fluid produced by a woman's body throughout the month reflects her reproductive health and overall wellbeing. A yoni that is healthy has a natural, pleasant odor and is self-cleaning. The yoni secretes clear or milky fluid to protect its sensitive and delicate tissues. However, when a woman is stressed, the pH level of her vagina can change from being naturally healthy and acidic to allowing alkaline organisms to breed. The stress hormones also thin out the mucous lining the yoni uses to protect itself from germs and bacteria that can cause disease.

Doing the cucumber cleanse, can help keep the yoni healthy and balanced. Cucumbers are very acidic, like the yoni, and naturally antiviral. They are more than 90 percent water (juicy) and contain many vitamins and cancer-fighting properties. Cucumbers also help to cleanse and purify the blood and are healing to the lungs, spleen, large intestines, and bladder.

Traditionally Tigresses would do this ritual once a week to maintain vaginal health, except when menstruating, of course.

Process

- It's simple. Get a cucumber about 8–10 inches long.

- Peel half of the cucumber, leave the other side with skin on to ensure you can grip it (you can slice it in half lengthwise as well, depending on how thick you want it).

- Insert the cucumber (I prefer the cucumber at room temperature, so keep in mind if you insert it after pulling it from the fridge, it will be cold).

- Twist the cucumber around inside the yoni and pull it in and out. This also massages the reflexology zones.

- Once you feel cleansed, remove cucumber. Try inserting your finger in your yoni and tasting your vaginal juices. Notice how it tastes now. It may be sweet or taste very "clean".

★Goddess Tip. Our yoni juice is a powerful source of pheromones, a chemical that attracts mates to us. You can dab some of your juice on you like perfume as an aphrodisiac.

Journal Reflection

1. How did it feel to do the cucumber cleanse? What did you notice about the way your yoni smelled and tasted afterward?

_____

_____

_____

_____

_____

2. Do you "dry" up when you're upset or tense? What ways have stress affected your juiciness?

_____

_____

_____

_____

_____

GODDESS MOON CYCLE

i bleed
every month.
but
do not die.
how am i
not
magic.
—Nayyirah Waheed, salt.

I'm sorry to tell you, but you've been fed a lie your whole life. Your menstrual cycle is not a curse. It is not unclean and shameful. It is holy, and you, my dear, are indeed magic.

Growing up, like many of you, I was raised with Christian dogma, which proclaimed that, because Eve ate some fruit God told her not to, she was cursed to experience pain during her childbearing years. This pain is supposed to be experienced by women through their menstrual cycle and childbirth.

I first got my cycle at age 11, and I was actually excited since many of the girls at school already had it. My mother thought I was weird. She told me about cramps which she suffered acutely from due to her endometriosis. I didn't care, I still wanted it, and when it came, I was happy.

That happiness soon turned to sadness as I experienced the dreaded menstrual cramps. I remember a couple of times in high school having cramps so bad I wished I would die. I remember thinking, "If I was to die right now, I wouldn't care!" It hurt so bad.

It has taken many years to recondition my body, mind, and womb so that I actually enjoy my sacred bleeding time. Through using the practices I've shared in this book, I have cured myself of dysmenorrhea (the medical term for period pain) and now experience a pain-free cycle. About 80 percent of women experience dysmenorrhea, so know that you are not alone if you do.

Ways to Have a Pain-Free Cycle

In Taoism, menstruation is referred to as "heavenly water", and it is considered sacred. It is life force, and as women, we lose *qi* while bleeding during our menses. Through practices like breast massage, yoni egg work, and Ovarian Breathing, you can lessen bleeding and menstrual pain by transforming blood into *qi*. Cramps are believed to be caused by cold contracted energy in the womb. Just like you shiver when you are cold, the womb "shivers," and these contractions trigger pain. The key to having a pain-free menstrual cycle is to keep energy moving in the womb and to have a warm, not cold, womb.

The Taoist practices mentioned above help to do that along with dancing - especially dance forms that bring energy to your core and pelvis like African dance, bellydance, twerking, gyrating, wining, etc.

Doing squats, yoga, and *qi gong* also all help to move energy in the body. It is also recommended to have a balanced diet that includes fresh fruits and vegetables, limiting processed and fast foods.

Taoists also believe that internal dampness stagnates like a swamp in the lower body and can cause cramps. To prevent cramps, avoid eating dampening foods like dairy, sugar, peanuts, and bananas for two weeks before your period. I have found that consuming dairy, sugar, and salt while on my cycle will make the cramps and feelings of heaviness worse. Eat light, warming foods like soups and stews.

Avoid cold foods like raw vegetables and salads, which causes more coldness to accumulate in the womb. While on your cycle, you can drink warming teas like ginger to bring warmth and nourishing teas like mugwort and red raspberry leaf to help balance hormones. You can use a heating pad or hot water bottle to also bring warmth to your womb.

Also, be sure that you are using natural products on your yoni during your cycle. Organic cotton pads must replace pads with chemicals, bleach, and synthetics. There are also other options like washable cloth pads and menstrual cups many women use that are very economical. Using products with chemicals for our most sacred place can throw our hormonal balance off and expose us to harmful chemicals.

Moon Time is Holy Time

Your cycle is your holy time, and the most important thing for you to do is actually to rest and allow your womb to release. In some cultures, while women were on their cycles, they would stay in separate huts called "moon lodges" or "red tents" where they would rest and have women who are non-menstruating serve them. Among certain Native American and African tribes, during their moon time, women were encouraged to retreat, not because they were unclean, but because they were at the height of their power. They were receptive to messages from the spiritual world. She was encouraged to spend time listening to her inner voice and come back with messages for the tribe.

Yurok, a native tribe from the northwest coast of the United States, had women who saw their periods as a time for purifying themselves. Many of the women were on a shared menstrual cycle and would do a series of rituals together. They believed it was when they had their most heightened spiritual experiences.

One of the greatest mysteries of feminine power lies in our connection to the moon. The macrocosmic cycle of nature, to ebb and flow, is played out in the bodies of women. For the ancients, the link between women and the moon was obvious. In the same way that the moon goes through a 28 or 29-day cycle of gaining power and energy to dwindling power and energy, so do our bodies.

The moon moves from the darkness of the New Moon to the height of its power during the Full Moon, to the subsequent waning.

Our bodies go through a cycle that expands beyond the 3 to 5-day menses but includes the entire four weeks of our fertility cycle. The moon interacts with the electromagnetic field of our bodies and affects our internal physiological process. This is why many dub a woman's menstrual cycle her holy moon time.

It is believed that when women spend sufficient time under natural light, we bleed during the New Moon and ovulate during the Full Moon.

Studies show that peak rates of conception occur at the Full Moon or the day before. During the New Moon, ovulation and conception rates decrease overall.

This is the cycle of creation, of life and death. We hold these mysteries in our bodies.

Your Moon Cycle is an Oracle

When we walk around knowing the innate power of our moon cycle, then it becomes an oracle: a way for us to connect with Spirit. In order to experience this power, you must rest as much as possible. Western culture has no red tents or moon lodges for women. We are expected to carry on with our normal daily duties and routines as if nothing is happening. We hide our bleeding time and function as if it is a regular day.

Very often, because our body is wise and knows she needs to be resting, we often experience heightened irritation and anger when having to interact with the outside world. This is because our bleeding time is the height of *yin* energy. This is a time to go within, not to be externalized and interacting with the outside world. Do your best to rest at this time. Train your children and partner to give you your space. If you can afford to, order out or prepare food ahead of time. Do your best to respect your body's natural process of release.

This is how your moon time becomes an oracle. If you are not still, you cannot hear the messages. It is my belief that when the womb opens, the heart opens. That's why you may experience such tender emotions during your moon time. Don't suppress them; let them get in touch with you and share their wisdom. When one has a clean diet, and the womb is not cold and contracted with stagnant, negative energy, the opening will be less toxic. Instead of feeling lots of irritation, you'll feel a heightened sensitivity to Spirit. This sensitivity will enable you to channel messages and receive divine revelations. Write, make art, sing, cry, and dance. This is a holy time. Anyone who tells you anything else is a liar.

Here are some exercises you can do during this time. Remember, this isn't about doing, it's about BEING! Stop. Drop. And bleed. Allow yourself to be and flow.

Moon Cycle Exercises

1. Journaling

Journaling is perhaps one of the most powerful things you can do while bleeding. You can journal about what you'd like to release. You can reflect on the moon cycle that is ending, your emotions, and anything that is coming up for you. Use the heightened sensitivity to get in tune with your deeper truths. What have you been suppressing all month that is coming to the surface now? There is a belief that our menstrual cycle is our "truth serum." We say or do things we may not be as open to say when not menstruating. What do you have to say?

You can also do stream of conscious writing, just letting the words flow on the page nonstop for a time without judging what is coming through. You can write poetry or sketch if you're an artist. I was a creative writing major in high school, and I noticed my writing was so much better when on my period. Allow your creative juices to flow onto the page.

2. Offer blood as a libation to the earth or houseplants

Our menstrual blood is life force and is filled with the nutrients that would have nurtured a baby. You can collect your blood in a menstrual cup, which is a reusable cup made of materials such as silicone. There are many different brands on the market now and you can research to find which one best fits your yoni.

Take the blood from the cup and add it to a larger cup you will keep for these purposes. Add water to it and use it as a libation or offering back to the earth. You can pour it into a houseplant or directly onto the ground if you have a backyard. Many believe that menstrual blood was, in fact, the first blood sacrifice of ancient times. As you pour, say prayers, and give thanks to Mother Earth for all she has blessed you with. Give thanks for the power and mystery of the divine feminine as expressed through your sacred moon cycle. Share what you would like to let go of at this time and what you would like to receive.

3. Anoint sacred objects and crystals with moon blood

Many ancient cultures saw a woman's menstrual blood as spiritually potent. The Cherokee believed that menstrual blood had the power to destroy one's enemies. Certain African tribes used it to empower their most potent charms. For religious ceremonies, Australian aborigines painted their sacred stones and themselves with red ochre, declaring that it represented women's menstrual blood.

You can use some of your menstrual blood to anoint and empower your sacred objects such as stones, crystals, statues, candles, etc. You can even dab a dot on your third eye to increase the power of your meditation.

4. Kidney Breathing

I shared in Week 3 how Kidney Breathing is a good exercise for you to do while menstruating. Another way to do Kidney Breathing is to lie on your back, either on the floor or your bed. Raise and bend your knees with feet flat on the floor or bed. Place your hands on your waist with your thumbs at the back, underneath the floating ribs. Gently press your thumbs into your kidneys.

As you inhale, feel your ribs expand, and your kidneys widen in the back, pressing into the surface below you. Imagine your kidneys expanding with the breath and being filled with blue light. You can say "Peace" to your kidneys, inviting them to relax. Exhale and let it go. You can also rub your hands warm and give yourself a kidney massage. Doing postures that open the kidneys and pelvis helps you breathe deeply and can alleviate menstrual cramps. You can relax in child's pose or squat while doing deep, slow breathing.

Avoid fast-paced exercises and cardio while on your moon time. These types of exercises will make you bleed heavier and deplete your energy even more. Do not overexert yourself physically; preserve your life force.

5. Womb Breathing

During your menstrual cycle is a beautiful time to connect with your womb through breathing and meditation. You can place your left hand on your heart and right hand on your womb (If you are a lefty, then it's the opposite). Receive warmth and love from your heart and send it down to your womb. See it traveling as a warm, pink light. You can send it down with the healing sound for heart "Haaaawww." Then switch and put your right hand on your heart and left hand on your womb. Breathe up any coldness from the womb to be transmuted by the fire of the heart.

6. Womb Massage

This is also a great time to do a womb massage. You can warm a carrier oil like almond or coconut and add an essential oil like rose, which has been found to help decrease anxiety and reduces inflammation that leads to menstrual cramping. Clary sage is another essential oil you can use that is a natural pain reliever. Massaging your abdomen will help blood naturally flow and bring warmth and comfort to the womb.

7. Womb Wrapping

You can wrap *qi* around your womb to help lessen bleeding and allow the womb to heal. This is good to do if you notice your cycle dragging on or spotting once it is done. Place your hands in an upside triangle on your womb, thumbs underneath the belly button. Breathe up earth energy into your womb. Earth energy rules the spleen, which helps to build the blood in Chinese medicine. Spiral earth energy counterclockwise through your womb. Imagine the wound healing. Feel your womb fill with a golden-yellow light.

SACRED SEX FOR COUPLES

When people recognize that they are spirit in a human body and that other people are spirits, they begin to understand that our bodies are sacred and that sexuality is far more than a means of pleasure; it is a sacred act. They look at other people differently, seeing the body not as a source of physical attraction but as a shrine.
—Sobonfu Some, The Spirit of Intimacy: Ancient African Teachings in the Ways of Relationships

Intention: Share in a sacred sex ritual with our partner.

While this section can be a book in itself (and fills the content of many books), I thought I'd share some additional ways you can bring sacred sex into the bedroom with a partner. I will not focus on different Kama Sutra–like sexual positions but instead on approaching intimacy with intention and opening to deeper, more spiritual sexual relations. As Sobonfu Some said, when we begin to see our lovers as shrines, the embodiment of the Divine on earth, our sexual connections will transform.

I am going to lay out a ritual of different sacred sexual practices you can do with your partner, combining both Tantric and Taoist techniques. Obviously, we will not be able to do a long ritual every time we want to have sex, but doing something like this even once a month with our partner will have a tremendous healing and bonding effect. An ideal time to practice sacred sex rituals is during the full moon. At that time, the energies of the earth are at their highest levels of receptivity, and vibrations are soaring high. It is a great time to energize a goal or intention, do healing work or open up to communion with the Divine.

You can apply different Tantric or Taoist sexual practices from time to time during regular lovemaking sessions. Remember that this is both an art and a science, but try not to get stuck in your head (men can have a lot of issues with this). As an artist, I say focus on the art, and the science will come with time. Let your intuition guide you and sometimes toss the entire technique out, invite Spirit in and be spontaneous. Let it be a dance!

Instructions for Maithuna or Dual Sexual Cultivation

Much of our work has been about cleansing and awakening our own sexual energy. Now we will focus on how these practices combine in our lovemaking with another. "Maithuna," meaning sexual union, is the word for the practice of daily lovemaking in Tantra.

Traditionally, this practice was done every day for one hour or more. In the Taoist tradition, various healing sexual positions were prescribed for several times a day. However, in these modern times, this is unrealistic for most of us. You and your lover may decide on a chosen time once a week or once a month to practice the sacred sexual rite.

It is also advised to do this ritual with someone that you have a strong foundation and loving partnership with. The form of relationship is up to you (monogamy, polyamory, open relationship, etc.). We have discussed how sexual energy is bonding, so be mindful of that when you decide to invite someone into this ritual. Only choose someone who honors and respects you as a goddess.

Also, in both Taoism and Tantra, these rituals were created to help balance sexual polarity between a man and woman. I recognize that all women who read this may not have a partner who is a man. Today we recognize masculine and feminine energy are expressed in many ways through a variety of genders. For the purpose of this ritual, your partner will represent the masculine and you the feminine. Feel free to improvise or edit in a way that suits your partnership.

Part 1: Ritual Prep

There are certain preparations that need to be made to ensure that our Tantric lovemaking is special and sacred.

Clean Environment

You should be sure that your house or bedroom is physically and energetically clean. Sweep, mop, and clear away clutter. Clutter attracts negative energy. Clean out your corners; negative energy can lurk there also. Clean your house spiritually with incense once you have cleaned it physically. You can burn sage, palo santo, or frankincense and myrrh, etc. Open a window and pass the incense through the house, mindfully asking all negative energy to leave and good energy to stay.

Clean Body

We all like to shower before our "boo" comes over, but we can add another level to this by doing a cleansing spiritual bath. There are certain herbs that are good to bathe with that cleanse your aura and are also easy to get, such as basil, rosemary, and mint. All herbs are best when fresh. Put cool water in a basin, wash off one or two bundles of each herb and place them in the water. Say your intentions/prayers as you tear the herbs into smaller pieces. You can add perfume or essential oils. Shower and pour the mixture over your body. Scrub with the herbs, let sit on your body for a couple of minutes and then rinse off. You can also revisit any of the baths from this book. Spiritual baths can be done alone or with your partner. You can bathe one another in rose petals, honey, and milk, for example. This can be beautiful erotic foreplay!

After you have bathed, you should dress in something soft and sensual with natural fibers, such as a silk robe or a cotton lappa. Adorn your body temple with scented oils, jewelry, and a little makeup. Waistbeads are particularly alluring. Looking like a god or goddess inspires a sense of worship from your partner. The vibration of metals and stones can also amplify your energy. Gold is solar (male), silver is lunar (female), and copper is earth (grounding). The combination of these brings a beautiful energetic balance.

Meditate

You may also do a short meditation before your lover comes. In your meditation, you can visualize how you'd like your sexual encounter to go. You can see yourself and your partner engaging in the ideal experience you'd like. You can also meditate on your heart and affirm your ability to give and receive love.

Set the Environment

Create an atmosphere that inspires lovemaking. Set up an altar dedicated to romance and love. Use a beautiful cloth draped over a table, add candles, and burn incense. Sandalwood is highly recommended for sacred sex rituals. You can also place crystals, erotic images, and books, symbolic statues, and figurines, flowers, etc. Maybe have something that symbolizes the love or relationship with your mate. Use your creativity. Feel free to have your partner help you in creating an altar.

Warm-Up the Body

Prior to the ritual, you can do light stretching to loosen up the body. Yoga and *qi gong* are great for this and will activate your energy centers. This is great to do together if they are open to this. It can help both of you relax and find new ways to be intimate. Don't be too serious and have a sense of humor about it. Help one another to stretch.

Part 2: Bonding and Energy Connection

In sacred sex, we don't just jump into sex. We need to spend time merging and bonding with our partner.

Eat Together

Spend some time talking to your partner and enjoying each other's company. Silence all distractions, including TVs and your phones. You can enjoy a small meal together. The following are traditional Tantric ritual foods. Each item has a symbolic meaning, and altogether, they represent the Universe.

Meat - represents the animal world and has a grounding energy (If you are vegan or vegetarian, use another protein source, so you have energy for lovemaking.)

Fish - symbolizes sexual energy and the element of water

Grain - stands for the earth and abundance

Fruit - brings the juicy sweetness of life

Red wine - represents the energy of life flowing through our veins

Cardamom seeds - each half of this seed represents the male and female aspects of being. They also make the breath sweet.

Eat, but do not stuff yourselves, as you won't have the energy for your union. Try placing the food mindfully in each other's mouth with intention, savoring each taste and morsel.

Sharing

As you talk to your partner, you can share what you are working on spiritually or what's happening in your life that you need healing around. You can also talk about what you want to manifest. This creates a context for the ritual. Each one of you knows what the other is working on. This information can be used during lovemaking and brings us closer.

Prayer

You and your partner can formally invite the Divine to be present during your union through a prayer or pouring of libation. Libation is a practice that comes from African traditions in which water is poured or sprinkled onto a plant, on the floor, or on an altar. You can call on your ancestors, whatever deities you work with, and/or Mother-Father God. Ask that your lovemaking be a divine offering bringing you deeper and closer into love. Ask for whatever you'd like to see healed or manifested. Invite Spirit to help you let go of whatever may be causing separation between you two.

Massage

Using massage can induce a trance-like state with your partner. As you touch certain energy points on the body, your *qi* starts to flow, kundalini awakens and begins to move through the chakras. Through massage, our partner can help balance the *yin* and *yang* aspects within us.

Massage Tips:

- The woman receives first. It is up to the man or masculine partner as the active energy to open her up.

- In the giving of the massage, a natural oil should be used like coconut, almond, or grapeseed oil. You can add essential oils if you like. Be sure to dilute with a carrier oil.

- You can begin by warming your hands and placing your sending hand—right hand (unless you're a lefty, then it's the reverse) on the coccyx at the base of the spine and your left receiving hand at the top of your partner's head. Feel the vibration in each center and the connection between them. These are our Shiva and Shakti centers.

- Once you send energy to connect these centers, focus on the lower back and work your way up. As a massage therapist, I've noticed most people carry tension in their back. The lower back is symbolic of feeling supported. When we have lower back pain, we often don't feel supported in life. Let your partner feel you supporting them and inviting them to relax.

- Pay special attention to the kidneys. Rub them awake, place both hands on their lower back and imagine blue energy going into their kidneys to stimulate the sexual energy.

- Tap and rub strongly at the sacrum to stimulate and awaken the kundalini.

- Stroke firmly on both sides of the spine, sending the energy up (do not put pressure directly on the spine, you don't want to endanger the spinal cord). You can also use your mouth to send warm air up the spine from the base to the neck. Breathe in through the nose and out through the mouth; you are creating a vacuum that draws energy up.

- Send your partner loving energy. Say healing prayers, chant, or sing over them.

Meditate and Breathe Together

Once both have massaged the other, you can sit naked in the Tantric *yab yum* position. The man or masculine partner sits cross-legged while the woman sits on his lap, legs crossed behind. You can use pillows or adjust where need be. Lightly touch your foreheads together, close your eyes and focus on the breath.

Start off by breathing together, in and out at the same time. After a few minutes of that, then you can share the breath. You breathe out; he breathes in. When he breathes out, you breathe in. By cycling your breath, you're cycling the energy. As you close your eyes, you can visualize the Microcosmic Orbit flowing between your bodies. This can be a very intimate and yummy practice. You may start to feel the energy circulate between you two naturally.

Affirm Your Intention

Here you will decide what the intention is for your lovemaking. Perhaps you want to work sex magic to accomplish a goal or manifestation. Maybe you desire healing around an issue that's been coming up between you two. You could also just want to surrender to pleasure and bliss. State what your intention is for your partner and yourself. Have him do the same.

Foreplay

From here, you can move into kissing and foreplay. When you kiss, be conscious of the connection of the four energy channels between you two (the *yin* and *yang* channels that begin and end in the mouth). Slow down and allow yourself to feel the sparks of electricity. Your partner should be sure to stimulate the breast to awaken the yoni, as the breasts are the woman's positive pole. Caress and lick each other's ears; remember they connect to the kidneys and have 120 energy points.

There is a Taoist saying that a woman's sexual energy is like a pot of water that must be made to boil. She needs a significant amount of time to reach arousal while men come hot and ready. Make sure you have a significant amount of foreplay so your waters can "boil." Many women do not reach orgasm because they aren't being aroused for long enough.

While you receive pleasure, do not shy away from giving. If your partner is a man, see giving fellatio as an empowering act. You have the opportunity to stimulate the reflexology zones of your partner's penis with your tongue and take him to the edge of ecstasy. He will be putty in your hands if you do it right. The White Tigresses of China used oral sex techniques to persevere their youthful appearance and reach the heights of spiritual orgasm.

Remember, on the head of his penis is the zone of the heart. Pay special attention to this area as well as his testicles (balls), the storehouse of his *jing*, and the perineum, the space between his genitals and his anus. Many men will go crazy when this spot is licked or stimulated. It can be more enjoyable than head itself. When you are sucking, you can contract your yoni to stimulate your own sexual energy as well as massage your breast. Imagine that he is giving you his most potent sexual life force. See it as a color filling your mouth, crown chakra, or even your entire body. Drink it into your lower tan tien and circulate it nine times.

There are many activities that can be added to the bonding section, such as dancing together, or you can do a sexy striptease for your partner. There are also different kinds of meditations you can do together. You can sit across from one another, gaze into each other's eyes softly and share energy that way. You can move a ball of *qi* through each other's Microcosmic Orbit. The possibilities are endless.

Part 3: Tantric Lovemaking

"Woman as the feminine, receptive force has the capacity to draw male energy upward through her vagina, as if raising it to a higher frequency. The vagina melts around the penis and drinks the energy radiating from it. When the penis and vagina are united in penetration, they form a complete unit, one dynamic force and one passive force, a live electromagnetic circuit."

—Diana Richardson, Tantric Orgasm for Women

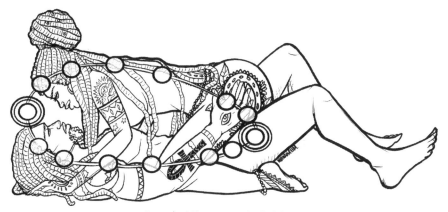

Couple Microcosmic Orbit

After foreplay has gone on for a satisfying amount of time and the woman is fully aroused, the man may enter her. Some Tantrikas say the man should ask permission to enter her sacred vessel and if she is ready to receive him. This is reflected in modern concepts of consent. In your own way, give permission for your partner to enter you. During lovemaking, the man is seen as Shiva, the divine masculine, and the woman is seen as Shakti, the divine feminine. Feel free to use whatever divinities you connect to. You could be Oshun, and he could be Ogun.

Tantra is a path of expansion through pleasure. During sexual intercourse, we allow ourselves to experience pleasure at higher and higher states. The sexual pleasure we experience is sublimated to bring healing and cleanse the pain we are carrying in our physical, emotional, and spiritual bodies.

During sex with our partner, the energy we experience is magnified three times as we bring our own energy, connect it to our partner's energy, and unite with our partner to create a third spiral of energy. This is what makes sacred sex so powerful.

During spiritual intimacy, we balance the *yin/yang*, or feminine and masculine energy within ourselves. The man or masculine partner becomes more passive and receptive; the woman becomes more dynamic and active. We feed one another the energy we need to balance ourselves through sexual union. A basic principle is the one who actively moves brings healing to the other lover, while the one who is more passive receives the healing. The inactive person can concentrate and feel their partner's sexual energy merge with theirs and circulate it through the Microcosmic Orbit. They can visualize a goal or send it to their organs for an organs orgasm.

Valley Orgasm vs. Peak Orgasm

Peak orgasm is what we are accustomed to having during sex. It involves a considerable amount of physical exertion that builds up tremendous tension and then is finally released. Most people's sexual intercourse does not last much beyond 15 minutes. This blame can particularly fall on the shoulders of the man who often peaks and ejaculates very easily.

In Tantra, the man has to train himself to maintain his seed as long as possible or "injaculate"; orgasm without ejaculating and recirculate his energy within himself for longer sustained love making. Now when you introduce this idea, some men will laugh at you and say it's impossible to orgasm and not ejaculate. However, it is very possible. He can begin practicing by bringing himself close to orgasm on his own without going over the edge several times. Then he can breathe the energy up through his own Microcosmic Orbit. He can also gradually learn to apply the locks or bandhas that you learned in the full-body orgasm exercise.

During intercourse, guide him to slow down when he feels close to ejaculation, breathe deeply, and apply the power locks (clench the toes, squeeze the perineum, tuck the tailbone, tighten the thighs, and buttocks, close the fists, and tuck the chin). When he releases the power locks, energy will shoot up his spine. He can then circulate it in his crown to feed his brain and higher spiritual centers. In learning this technique, if a man does ejaculate, he has still absorbed some of his life force and circulated it to feed his body, rather than just release it through ejaculation. His ability to last for a longer time will allow both of you to reach more intense pleasure.

Sacred sex focuses on valley orgasm, which involves building excitement in our partner, allowing the energy to decrease when close to orgasm, and then building it again and again. Each time, not allowing the other to fall over the edge, but experience a sort of suspended orgasmic peaceful state.

The idea is that with each build, we bring each other into higher and higher orgasmic states. Both of you can use the power locks simultaneously: feel the energy shoot up into the crown chakra and circulate it there nine times or so, and exhale it down. You can also send the sexual energy through each chakra, seeing the color of that chakra as you move it up from the root to the crown.

During our valley, we can focus on letting it go and noticing what spontaneous orgasmic sensations we have. During the "rest" portion, we can also concentrate on our goals. Our partner can "seed" us with visions that bring healing or align with what we desire to manifest. (For example, "Yes honey, I see you getting that promotion at work," etc.) As we transmute our energy into the higher spiritual centers, we may see visions or hear messages from the spiritual realm. This is making sex a meditation.

A guideline for awareness during sex can go like this:

1. **Physical:** Complete focus and giving in to the physical pleasure in the moment. The key is to surrender, give and receive.

2. **Emotional:** Feeling loving thoughts and connecting to your partner. The key is to open your heart and be vulnerable.

3. **Spiritual:** Seeing our partner and ourselves as one unit connected to the Spirit. The key is to acknowledge you and your mate's divinity.

Once peak climax does happen, you can choose to try to focus on bringing the energy up to the crown chakra, intensely visualizing your goal and releasing it into the Universe or just completely surrendering to the "little death." The key to women being orgasmic is to be totally relaxed. Remember you don't have to work hard. If your partner orgasms, allow yourself to also absorb their sexual energy. This can trigger orgasmic waves and pulses in your own body. Very often, when a partner of mine orgasms, it is like I've had another orgasm, and their energy moves through me in ripples.

Once you have finished your ritual, you may share any visions that you saw or messages you heard during the experience. This can be done the next morning, of course, if you just want to lay together in total orgasmic bliss.

MY FIRST TIME: A SACRED SEX SHORT STORY

9 pm. Butterflies did the Harlem Shake in my stomach. He was on his way any minute now. I was dressed in all white, ready to go. Part of me thought I must be crazy. Really? Are you inviting a man you never met over to your house, who you only talked to on the phone?!!! Not only that, but you found him on Facebook!! The theme from Halloween played in my head... Dododododododododo! He could be an axe murderer for all you know! I had seen his pictures, and he was tall. Very tall. Not sure how tall, but he seemed to tower over everyone else in his photos. So not only was I inviting a stranger to my house, but he was a tall stranger. Ok, I know I'm crazy. This is what you are told not to do on all the websites and after-school specials.

Well, he wasn't a complete stranger. I mean, he was known by my people. People I trusted who knew him very well. So, call it naivety, stupidity, or a gut instinct, but I somehow trusted that everything would be ok. That inviting this stranger to my house on a Tuesday night to take our "test" together was safe. Perhaps it was the warm smile Jelani had in all his photos, the fact that one of my girlfriends actually worked for him in his acupuncture office, or the solid base in his voice that cooed me into feeling it was just fine. The "test" we were taking, however, wasn't just some ordinary exam; it was a Tantric exam...

Tantra, an ancient mystical practice from India, had my nose wide open for some time. Several years earlier, when I was married, I remember stumbling upon it in one of my spiritual books. I read about women going into trance while making love to their lovers and being able to give them messages from the spiritual realm. This blew my mind. I highlighted and dog-eared that page, thirsty to get more information. The idea of connecting my sexuality to my spirituality touched something within me, like a warm hand reaching under my skirt. I was slightly hesitant but intrigued, desiring to find out more. When I brought it up to my then-husband, he was not really feeling it; the idea of sex and spirit weirded him out. But now, three years out of the marriage, I was free to explore it on my own.

I enrolled in a six-month online class that met in cyberspace monthly to explore Tantric principles and techniques. In this course, I learned that sex is actually only ten percent physical intercourse and ninety percent other ways of connecting and pleasing our partners. I learned that our orgasmic potential was infinite, especially for women, and that there were many different types of orgasms. Deeper still, I learned that orgasmic energy was, in fact, healing energy and that we could use the ecstasy of physical orgasm to manifest goals in our life and feel the illumination of transcendence.

Up until now, we had been studying the theory, and now was time to practice! We needed a person of the opposite sex to practice with. The methods we were studying used feminine and masculine energy to balance each other, so men brought healing to women and vice versa. Dating but single at the time, I did not have a lover available to perform my Tantric test on. So when I discovered that one of the men taking the class was also the boss of one of my girlfriends, I Facebook-friended him and asked him if he'd like to complete the test with me. Since we were both in New York, we'd gain the advantage of practicing with one another. He was also a doctor of the ancient science of Chinese acupuncture, so it seemed a perfect fit. After I inboxed him, we had a couple of phone conversations and agreed we'd "test" with each other. He seemed so gentle and knowledgeable with a voice that was deep and smooth as silk...

It was all so serendipitous. So why was I so nervous? For me, Tantra had just been alive in my imagination and within the pages of my books. I was really just a nerd with a vivid imagination, but now things were becoming three-dimensional. Of course, sexual intercourse was not on our "test"; it only involved moving sexual energy in a very subtle way that, once certified, we could do with our clients who would be perfect strangers. It was more akin to massage and Reiki.

At 9:21 pm, he called me, "Hey, I just got out the subway. Be there in 5 minutes."

"Ok, see you soon," I responded.

Gulp, it was happening. I looked in the mirror to make sure I looked fine. Well, not that I was trying to be attractive. This wasn't a date or anything. Tantra is really spiritual; I kept telling myself. I was wearing all white as we were told in class to neutralize our energy and invoke a sense of peace. But I had to make sure nothing was in my teeth. In meeting someone for the first time, one had to make a good impression. Smile Shepsa. Good, teeth clean. My long Senegalese twist cascaded down my back; I used a hair tie to bring it away from my face so I could work with an unobstructed vision. I wore a short sleeve V-neck white t-shirt and a long, flowy white skirt that almost covered my feet.

Oh-uh, no bra! Taking off my bra as soon as I got home was a routine practice of mine. I hated bras and loved the freedom of feeling my breast move unrestricted. But I have super nipples, and they can't help but poke out like fingertips through my shirt if I'm braless.

I heard a knock on my door. Shit! He was here, no time to try and find my bra. Oh, well. This is my house; I deserve to be comfortable. I went to open the door to the garden floor brownstone apartment I rented and felt a burst of the cold, bitter December air. I saw his long frame in the shadows and quickly welcomed him in to escape the winter chill. I scurried inside, closing the door behind us, and got my first good look at him. The pictures did not lie; he was tall. Very tall, well over six feet, but he was buried beneath his winter coat and hat. I tried not to stare and be a good host. No one that tall had ever been in my home.

"Hey, Jelani, nice to meet you. Let me take your coat."

He pulled off his long brown coat, and I hung it on a hanger in the closet. Then I could truly see him. Despite being tall, he had a youthful look; clear cocoa brown skin, close-cut black hair with a slight curl, the same gentle eyes as in his pictures, and a moustache that curled over his lips in a smile that made me blush.

"So this is you, huh? Lady Shepsa." He leaned his body over, almost seeming to bend in half to give me a hug. Despite us having just met, there was something so familiar about him.

"This is me," I said, wrapped in his arms. He had a very strong embrace; I wilted just a little. Being hugged by someone that tall made me feel like a little girl. This was very different for me as I stand at 5'9, which is tall for a woman. "Come on in. Did it take you long?" He came inside from the hallway, and we sat on my couch.

"No not at all. Actually, being around here brought back memories. I used to live not too far away."

"Oh really?"

"Yes, my family lived over here when I was a kid."

"I'm sure it looked different back then. Bed-Stuy has now become Stuyvesant Heights with condos and doormen and sidewalk cafes."

"Yes, I know. Harlem is the same way. But we still there, holding on strong."

"Or something." I chuckled. "I love Brooklyn, though; the culture is so alive. How do you like Harlem? I've never lived there."

"Oh, I love Harlem. That's where my practice is. I get to walk to work. The culture is still there too. I always wanted to open up a practice there."

"Really, why?"

"It's been my vision since I was a teenager. Harlem is very historical for our people. So much history. I always had a vision of practicing acupuncture there. It's one of the hearts of Black America."

"I don't go to Harlem often, but when I do, it's cool being there. The work you do sounds amazing. I had acupuncture once a few years ago."

"You should come by my practice sometime." Jelani smiled a warm invitation.

"I'd love to." A voice inside said, *Yeah, I'd love to have you stick needles in me.* No! Stop Shepsa! This is innocent. Be serious! The butterflies in my stomach were now doing a pole dance.

"Do you mind if I use your bathroom? I want to change; I came straight from work."

"Oh, yes, sure. I didn't realize the time, it's almost time to begin. Come this way."

I led him to the bathroom so he could change his clothes. I went into my bedroom to light the candles. The crazy thoughts started kicking up again. Am I really going to invite this man into my bedroom so he can work tantrically on me? Correction, am I really going to invite this fine, tall man into my bedroom to swirl around my sexual energy? I felt the blood rush to my face as I thought about it. He came out of the bathroom, interrupting my thoughts.

"Where can I put my things?"

Startled, I turned around, almost dropping the match I used to light my yellow and pink candles. He looked like a Nubian God standing there in all white. I could see his taut muscles slightly flexed underneath his white shirt.

"Oh, right here." I replied, pointing to a chair. I tried to be as relaxed and informal as possible. We got into the business of setting up the laptop and signing on to our class. We would be led, step by step, by our instructors on what to do. Jelani had some *nag champa* incense and lit it; the air smelled like an Indian palace or maybe a Tantric temple...

10 pm. It was time for our class. It was amazing and kind of funny to me that some of these ancient Tantric teachings could be learned virtually. The beauty of technology! We had a male and female instructor that would lead us through the practice. It was established that I would receive healing energy first. Whew! Because I didn't have a massage table, I laid face up on my bed and proceeded to receive healing from Jelani, my Tantric partner.

"Just breathe deeply and relax." His voice poured over me like honey; his energy felt warm and nurturing, like a good doctor. He led me through some deep breathing for about five minutes and used a special blend of oil that smelled of frankincense as he waved his hands up and down my body without touching me. At first, I just felt relaxed as I focused on my breathing. Then slowly, I could feel the sexual energy being emitted from his hands.

I started to let out small moans as he worked on me energetically. Though my eyes were closed, I could sense when he was focusing on different areas of my body, even without him actually touching me. Some parts felt warm; others felt cold. I could feel a sweet sensation moving around in my pelvis that made me curl my toes. Sensual waves flowed down my arms, and just when it seemed to be getting really good, it was time to stop and switch.

He laid his long body on my bed. I closed my eyes and steadied myself, still reeling somewhat from my experience. I then began my energy work on him. Because of the nature of men being more physical, needing touch, our Tantric technique involved me actually touching his chest and using gentle massage to stimulate his sexual energy. After unsuccessfully trying to reach across the bed to work on him, I straddled my legs around his waist and began to give my massage in a more direct manner.

While it felt great to receive, it was also nice to give. I closed my eyes and breathed deeply, sending loving healing energy into the places I sensed he needed most. I became startled as he actually began to let out loud moans and growl-like sounds. Using my intuition, I sensed what he might need to do in his actual life to balance his energy. I saw visions of Jelani walking in the forest. I began to intuit he would be very spiritually fed by going out into nature, someplace with trees.

When my turn was over, all the students had a virtual discussion of what our experiences were giving and receiving energy. I shared that it was my first time feeling orgasmic energy in my body without physical touch. I also shared what I sensed that Jelani might need additionally to add more balance to him. He found my insight about going out into nature very insightful. When it was his turn to speak about what it was like to receive, he was almost lost for words.

"I-I never felt anything like that before..." He let out a booming laugh that seemed to shake my walls. "My hands, my arms. I could feel---I-I-I...Yeah, it was special. I never felt anything like that." His reaction stupefied me. Little ol' me? He felt like that from little ol' me? Whoa... Maybe there was something to this Tantric stuff...

Our class wrapped up, and my stomach was growling. I had cooked some food before Jelani arrived but had not eaten because I didn't want to practice on a full stomach. Being a polite host, I invited Jelani to stay for a late-night dinner before he headed back to Harlem.

"Hey, I cooked some food. Are you hungry? It's nothing big. Just some lentils, kale, and brown rice. Boring but healthy."

"No that sounds great. I am actually starving."

While we ate, I felt more relaxed. No longer was I having crazy thoughts; I felt completely safe with this man. It was almost as if we met before. Over dinner, we cracked jokes and laughed; it seemed like we had known each other for years. I was so impressed with his spiritually knowledgeable yet down-to-earth vibe. We both shared an interest in traditional African religions. Noticing some cowrie shells on my altar, he explained to me the Yoruba divination system of obi.

"When two of the cowries' shells are facing up, and two are facing down, that's *ejife*. It means the way is balanced and open..." And so on, he went sharing his spiritual knowledge.

The way he did it made me feel so erotic. He pointed out that the cowrie shells actually looked like yonis, the Sanskrit word for vagina, and the oracle was based on the balance of masculine and feminine energy. Enlightened men were extremely sexy to me. My butterflies were now stripped naked. Growing tired, I laid across my bed as we talked, and he sat on the edge. He reached out and lightly touched my calf. "Is it ok if I do this...? This is your spleen energy meridian". I nodded yes. He gave my leg a light caress... the energy shot straight to my heart.

1 am. After all our talking, we both decided it was too late for him to travel back to Harlem. "I could sleep on your couch if that's ok with you." Jelani said.

"Ummmm, you can't fit on my couch!" I laughed, then curiously asked, "How tall are you anyway?"

"Only 6'8."

That's a lot of man.

"Nonsense, you can sleep in my bed. I trust you... The couch hurts my back, so we'll just have to share."

"Ok."

Now you're bugging!! You're letting him stay over and in your BED!! You're asking for trouble... Ignoring "the voice" I laid under the covers, still wearing my whites. My room was dark other than the dance of the yellow candlelight. Jelani was in the living room doing some *qi gong* and yoga, his nightly routine, he told me.

As I waited in the bed, I began to feel hot. I really, really just wanted his body next to mine. Fuck it; I wanted him, all 6'8 of him all over me! He seemed to be taking forever with his exercise. What kind of man does yoga and *qi gong* before going to bed? Duh! A man you want! I tried to go to sleep but I couldn't. I didn't want the night to be over yet...

After what seemed like forever, he came and laid down next to me. His body felt warm and only made me hotter. There was a silence that was not awkward but thick like air inside a steam room. It was as if the quiet was speaking the words we dare not say. My body was screaming for him to touch me. Breaking the silence, Jelani said something totally unexpected...

"You know I usually sleep naked."

I burst out in nervous laughter. "So why don't you..."

"I thought about it, but...I don't want to scare you."

"What you think? You'd be the first naked man I've ever had in my bed?"

"It was a joke."

Silence again...

I went from being hot to feeling out of control. I actually think I became possessed. My entire body was calling for this man, and I felt like he was teasing me. How could he discuss being naked and not touch me? He was playing games...

"You're probably the first man in my bed who's never kissed me."

Being a Pisces, it wasn't my nature to make the first move. I refused to grab his face and kiss him. We fish are more subtle, preferring to attract... besides, I wanted to feel his desire for me.

"Well... I did think about it." He whispered. He was lying on his back, looking up at the dance of shadows on the ceiling from the candlelight. His face seemed serious. I leaned in closer to him.

"What happened?"

"I didn't think it would be right." Something in me grew fierce. This man was going to touch me! I began rubbing my leg against his.

"Oh, now you're playing..."

"I don't know what you're-" His lips swallowed whatever words I was trying to get out. The levy of passion broke open between us, and we became swept away in the flood. He went from being on his back to being between my legs. All six foot eight of him laced his body on top of me. Surprisingly, he did not feel heavy, nor was I overwhelmed. It was as if he was flowing into me. He smelled of earthy myrrh and frankincense, the oil he used in our Tantra session.

As his lips tasted mine, he put his hands on my hips and pulled me closer to him. I wrapped my legs around his waist. He kissed me like he wanted to devour me, and I let out ecstatic moans, happily being consumed. Moving from my mouth, he began savoring my neck, eventually moving down to explore the rest of me. Cupping my breasts in his hands, he gently licked my nipples; I lit up like a tree on Christmas Eve. I felt orgasmic energy in every pore of my body. It was as if my skin wanted to drink him. I never wanted anyone as much as I wanted him in that moment...

As if sensing that my entire body was calling him, he began to kiss me all over, letting out growl-like sounds and moans of satisfaction. It was as if he enjoyed pleasing me as much as I enjoyed being pleased.

"Oh my god... your skin... your taste... your smell." He inhaled me.

Was this how it felt to be worshipped? It was as if he couldn't get enough of me, and I knew he was flooded with the same energy I felt too. Like a ravished hunter ready to dine, he grabbed my legs and pulled my yoni closer to his mouth. He painted my clit with his warm wet tongue. But he did not just stop there; my yoni lips also received his masterful art. His tongue went deep diving inside my pulsating walls, and he alternated with his finger massaging my g-spot. It felt so good;

I almost wanted to pull away. Feeling my tension, he held me closer, and I was forced to surrender. I came, and he happily tasted my juices. Almost immediately afterward, he was kissing my other lips, and I could taste me in his mouth. Something about that completely turned me on, when with other men, I might have been disgusted. I felt so open with him.

He wasn't done with me; he flipped me on my stomach. It was as if my entire body was a yoni as he began to kiss and lick up and down my spine. Is this what kundalini feels like? I could feel the energy surging up my back as if my spine was one long clitoris. I couldn't believe I was feeling this way and this man hadn't even penetrated me! The funny thing was, I did have a sexual partner at this time, a man named Kenneth. In fact, I had great love for Kenneth, yet I had never felt this way with him. With Jelani, I felt desire for him in every cell of my body and orgasmic waves that pulsated through my entire being. In the case of Kenneth, my sexual pleasure seemed to be located primarily in my genitals, and while it was good, it wasn't this good. I felt like he wanted me to perform for him. I did most of the work while he laid back and "took it." With Jelani, I completely surrendered into the fire of his passion. This wasn't him "fucking" me either like the porn stars try to do. This was completely something else. This was the god worshipping the goddess...

4 am. At some point, our eyes finally gave in to sleep. I felt like I was wrapped in a warm, golden light as I lay in his arms, feeling completely connected and safe. I had just had the most amazing sexual experience of my entire life. It was church, and my body was the altar, Jelani was the sermon, and we both were the primal choir sending our voices to heaven. He was gentle yet strong from start to finish - well, not really

finish because he never ejaculated. He practiced the Taoist method of injaculating: orgasming without releasing his seed.

When he entered me, he paid close attention to how I was feeling, careful not to hurt me with his long powerful penis. As he was inside of me, he told me I was beautiful. Now, I've had plenty of men tell me I was beautiful to get the pussy, but never one tell me I was beautiful while inside the pussy. I've heard sexy, but beautiful was something else... It made me feel like moonlight, like Oshun covered in sunflowers...

7 am. My eyes opened as I woke up to the sound of my phone alarm. I had no desire to get out of bed and leave the embrace of this cocoa king. The alarm awakened him too. We laid together for a moment, floating between being half awake and asleep. It hurt to try to get up when I barely got any sleep, but it hurt even more, to have to leave this experience behind and go on with the rest of my day like normal. Suddenly, as if reading my thoughts, Jelani started working on my body again. He kissed me all over. I never had a lover I felt comfortable kissing first thing in the morning – not even my ex-husband. I always thought it would be gross, but with Jelani, it wasn't. It was as if we were finishing where we left off previously. He even worshipped my yoni again with his tongue. Teasing me, telling me, "You know you don't have to go to work..." I had always been shy about my body after sex, thinking I needed to run to the shower, but Jelani happily had me for breakfast just as I was. He seemed to revel in my natural scent and flavors, turning me on with his growls. As the time ticked on, I knew I would be late for work if I didn't get out of bed.

"I-I-I have to go..." I pleaded but he only continued to massage my body with his strong hands and nibble moans out of my flesh.

"Do you?" he teased.

How I wish I could call out from work, but it was already too late. I longed to spend a day with him wrapped around me, but it would have to be another time.

"Ahhhhh... yes, I do. Let me get in the shower. I can't be late..."

"Ok," he acquiesced. "I don't want you to be late." He pulled his long body off me. I drunkenly got up, still dizzy with ecstasy. I stood before him, as naked as the day I was born, looking at his beautiful brown body spread over my bed. He looked like the sunrise.

I tried to walk to the bathroom when I was swooped up from behind. Jelani picked me up like I was a bag of feathers. I guess I would be late to work after all.

STAY *WET*! CONCLUDING THOUGHTS

Wow! You did it! You took 30 days to get *WET*! Thank you for joining me on this journey of deep-diving into sensual bliss and feminine pleasure.

If you haven't already, I invite you to join my community of women doing the work of reclaiming both our sacred *and* our sexy!

I offer a course that accompanies this book that has supporting videos for certain exercises, monthly Q&A calls, and live rituals. My journey to awakening my inner goddess became amplified when I began to learn from teachers and found a community of other women for support. You do not have to walk this alone. I would love to support you.

Visit https://letgoletgoddess.com/ to find out more about upcoming classes, live workshops, rituals, and the accompanying course for this book. You can also download my free Badass Goddess Juju Bundle that features meditations, affirmations, and rituals to help you step into your goddess power.

I invite you to stay *WET*! Use this book to reclaim your sacred, sexy self. Pleasure is medicine. Being orgasmic is your birthright!

Continue to make connecting to the goddess in you a daily practice. No matter what crazy may be swirling around in the world, you have the power to create your own sacred temple. Light some incense, pull out the candles, grab your oil. Massage your breasts and remember who you are!

"Caring for myself is not self-indulgence. It is self-preservation, and that is an act of political warfare"
—Audre Lorde

Periodt.

ACKNOWLEDGMENTS

I am because WE ARE! I am so grateful for every teacher I have had and every experience that has guided me onto this path of healing through sacred sexuality and divine feminine energy.

First, I would like to acknowledge my ancestors. I am thankful for their sacrifices and ability to survive the unthinkable, the Transatlantic Slave Trade, and the continuous assaults on our humanity so I could be here today. I am especially grateful for my badass ancestress, my mother, Theolia Jones (ibae). Thank you for guiding and protecting me from the other side, and yes, I will work on having more fun!

I would like to acknowledge Dr. Sunyatta Amen for exposing so many Black and Brown girls to the jade egg and the concept of sacred sexuality.

I am grateful to Ra Un Nefer Amen and the Ausar Auset Society, where I first learned about Taoism, the Five Elements, *qi gong*, and the I-Ching over 15 years ago.

I am abundantly thankful to Mantak Chia, who brought the teaching of Healing Love to the Western world and the work of Universal Healing Tao.

I was blessed to work personally with Minke de Vos and Shashi Solluna as my instructors in the Tao-Tantric Arts. Thank you for bringing the dance of the sacred feminine and the fusion of Taoism and Tantra to the world and empowering many other women to do so.

I am grateful to my teachers at the Swedish Institute, where my love for Taoism and Eastern healing became even more grounded during my massage therapy studies.

I am grateful to the work of Kenya K. Stevens and JujuMama LLC., where I learned so much about sacred sexual energy and relationships.

I am also grateful for the work of people like Michael Winn, Dr. Saida Desilets, and Sunyata Saraswati.

I am grateful to all the numerous healers, priests, and priestesses from India, China, and Africa, whom many of us will never know their names, but we benefit from their work and sacred lineages.

Last but not least, I am grateful to Oshun, for this is the answer to my prayers all those many years ago when I asked you to show me the secrets of being a woman. Modupe Oshun! Ore ye ye o!

ABOUT THE AUTHOR

Lady Shepsa Jones is a teacher, author, life coach, mother, and "juju woman"—one who taps into her magical powers for healing and manifestation. As a sacred femininity healer, she helps women who feel non-orgasmic, shut down and overburdened with the stressors of life, find bliss and fulfillment through connecting with their sacred sexual energy and divine feminine power.

She has spent over ten years studying the spiritual sciences of the African Diaspora, China and India. Through the study of Tantra and sacred sexuality, Shepsa has reconnected to the goddess within her and assists other women to do the same in her coaching programs and retreats. She is a published author of three other books, a poetry book called the *Goddess Pages: Honey, Full Moon and Daggers* and two self-help books for women called, *Happy and Healed, Five Steps to Getting Over ANY Man and Finding the Love You Deserve* and *Nice For What?! How To Go From Being A Good Girl To A Badass Goddess.*

Lady Shepsa is a certified yoga teacher and certified Sacred Femininity Facilitator from Tao Tantric Arts. Shepsa is also a licensed massage therapist. Through her company *Let Go Let Goddess*™, she guides women on a journey to their highest self, their inner goddess to discover a life of bliss.

CONNECT WITH ME

Thank you for reading my book. Please feel free to leave a review on Amazon.

Let's stay in touch!

Website

http://letgoletgoddess.com/

Facebook

https://www.facebook.com/LetGoLetGoddess

YouTube

Let Go Let Goddess

Instagram

@letgoletgoddess

Made in United States
Orlando, FL
10 September 2024

51349137R00136